sticks
stones
mud
homes

sticks stones mud homes
Natural Living

nigel noyes

design & art direction
simone aylward

Hardie Grant Books

If

we understand that
design
leads to the
manifestation
of human intention

and if what we make with our hands is to be

sacred

and
honour the earth that gives us life,

then the things we make
must not only rise from the ground
but return to it,
soil to soil,
water to water,
so
everything
that is received from the earth can be freely given back
without causing harm to any living system.

this is
ecology

this is
good design

It is of this we must now speak.

FROM A CENTENNIAL SERMON TITLED 'DESIGN ECOLOGY ETHICS AND THE MAKING OF THINGS'
WILLIAM McDONOUGH[1]

7 FEBRUARY 1993

contents

living environments

There is a
fascinating diversity
in how we live, from the
tight confines
of inner-city
one-room boxes to
expansive
accommodation
on isolated
rural retreats.

Whatever the location or scale of our current dwelling, there is always the opportunity to enhance this space into something we can genuinely refer to as home. A place where we can relax, feel grounded and stay in touch with our inner selves and our families – surroundings that encourage spiritual connections, stimulate and revive the senses, and help us regain vital energies.

Sticks, Stones, Mud Homes – Natural Living is designed to help you achieve such a place, and then kindle your interest in environmentally sensitive ways to create it. Looking at other people's inspirational spaces can invite us to embrace the whole process of making a home, with an informed and well-grounded sensibility. This book aims to pass on the means to plan our own holistic charter for living, founded on a collective responsibility for the environment.

The photographs in this book feature lived-in houses that illustrate how good design and sound building principles can combine to have less impact on the earth, and how ecologically sustainable development can be stylish, comfortable, economical and, of course, good for the environment.

9

past informs the future

Progressive designers, architects and builders have looked to many sources, including past cultures, to examine materials and construction methods that have proven successful over hundreds of years. Around the world venerable ideas and 'lost' skills are being revived – adapted to work with today's technology. Regional architecture, developed by trial and error over long periods, also offers insight into how to work with local climate conditions. Many of the owners featured in this book have used alternative methods of construction with an appreciation of the most basic building blocks – **earth, straw, timber and stone** – which form a natural alliance with the land. Some, in a pioneering spirit, have revived ancient building techniques, rescuing ideas from the past and combining them with contemporary technology for living today. Others have breathed new life into the old and pre-used by recycling. The merits of each of these building methods are looked at by chapter. The final chapter of the book explores the eco-potential to be found in the humblest of today's mass-produced materials.

spatial relationships

While the featured homes offer an eloquent visual and philosophical logic for considering 'radical' and reused materials in our structures, we can also draw inspiration from their variations in layout. A number of factors influence the planning of space, including lifestyle preferences and aims to reduce energy consumption. We can see that the siting and orientation of rooms **works with the climate** – the

principles of passive solar heating. There are valuable ideas on areas that we might want to emphasise – kitchens, bathrooms, studios and gardens – and innovative ways with which to **dissolve boundaries** between interiors and the world outside. The motivation behind these spatial arrangements often increases positive ambience and comfort while reducing energy demands.

inner thoughts

Establishing healthy rooms with ecological function can be a stimulating, often playful activity. In one house, ceilings reveal their straw insulation as a finish, enhancing acoustics and adding texture, while in another, panelling with reused timbers adds natural pattern and warmth. Colours are chosen to soothe or stimulate – careful thought given to their content and how they are applied. Owners select furnishings for physical and emotional comfort – some pieces carry memories of people and places. Rooms are shaped by their occupants' **inner thoughts and visions**, and objects gathered for their intrinsic beauty, spiritual connection or just on a whim. Interiors can reflect the personality traits of their creators – eccentricity, humour, pride, determination and ingenuity on display.

The houses featured are **resourceful** living environments put together by people who have clearly given long

thought to lifestyle and family requirements, linking their needs with a regard for the land. The results are living spaces full of character, nourished by creativity, soul and intuition, invariably bearing the natural imprint of a hands-on approach and often breaking a few rules in the process. The architectural gamut runs from a bush retreat, shaped with elementary materials found on-site, to the crafted refinement of a suburban family's straw bale home. Sharing in their diversity an **eye for good design** and a commonsense approach to living, all are imbued with spirit, all show sensitivity to their surroundings and all empower us by example to be eco-minded with a variety of resources – to furnish our retreats with integrity. A gentler, self-questioning approach can also add heart and soul to our homes – it is through these spaces and the way we choose to live that we **express our identity**.

If you have found your dream plot of land and entertain visions of a moated sanctuary, or you merely intend small-scale alterations to a rented room in the city, take a leaf or two from the thoughtful strategies throughout this book and transform your surroundings into something more harmonious and healthy.

develop

your own

sustainable

language for living

social changes

Before assessing our individual needs and determining how to go about shaping ecologically safe havens to nurture them, it is worth pausing to consider the continuing social changes that inform our lifestyles. The increased pace of life in a technology-led, global community has had a major **impact on living**, especially in developed countries. We notice added complexity in the workplace, computers driving changes in the way we do business and altering our social structure. The trend towards more flexible work hours often leads to work encroaching on previously designated leisure time. Our homes can also reflect these changes. Many of us now work or run a business from where we live, and have to make space for work activities and the equipment that goes with them. Some operate a portable office – often from a vehicle, or anywhere, in fact, we can rest a laptop or wield a mobile phone – saving on fixed overheads perhaps, but invariably turning other people's homes and commercial premises into work sites. There is an anxiety that accompanies these **changing work patterns**. We expect to be contacted, and to contact others, at almost any time, and are faced with intrusive pressures from a wide range of communication systems. For many people, particularly those who spend long working hours cramped in unhealthy and demanding inner-city environments, the restorative end-of-the-day 'antidote' is missing. A healing space is essential to help us cope with these demands. So what are the key factors to consider when preparing somewhere to revive the senses and what criteria should we apply to live responsibly in this century?

the decorative paper trail

Of course, there is no shortage of information on how we might create the 'perfect home'. Wherever we live, our local newsagent is sure to stock a plethora of architecture and decor magazines offering 'helpful hints' and veiled endorsements for 'indispensable' household items. Houses of the rich and famous – presumed aspirational – are laid open for inspection with roomscapes dominated by giant TV screens and garden areas devoted to swimming pools. The guidelines for fashionable decor are persuasive: we are offered solutions to our **craving** for the 'right' coffee table and warnings about the hazards of decorating with, say, 'notoriously difficult shades of purple' – advice for this season's colour palette usually necessitating another trip to the paint shop.

Real strategies for sustainable and healthy living are thin on the page. Rare and welcome are those publications that might **further the creation** of eco-friendly houses, promote the durability of 'green' materials and inform us about non-toxic finishes.

The trail of misinformation continues on popular television programs. 'Overnight' makeovers of our indoor and outdoor spaces are supervised by celebrity designers – seen grinning through the dust from their hasty labours. We watch unsuspecting owners return from a weekend away to greet these miracle transformations and indicate their 'delight' with transformations that often bear no reflection on their personality or values. Home improvements

are generally viewed as a means of leveraging house values – even the machinations of real-estate sales and auction rooms are seen as entertainment. Viewers are **encouraged** to present their antiques and family heirlooms for authentication by experts, as if price and provenance might help us fathom personal response to a piece. Our houses and their contents have been misappropriated as a trading commodity – their value expressed in dollars, square metres and superficial appearance. It is no surprise that mainstream media have a vested interest in depicting 'home making' as a **fashionable** activity, encouraging makeshift decor and unsustainable building practices – the pursuit of profit overshadowing **environmental cost**.

encouraging signs

Yet as this powerful media sector hard-sells a decorative **veneer** of civilised living, a core band of independent publishers, broadcasters and educational bodies seeks to inform. These independents are part of a 'counter' global network that includes internationally allied groups, government-funded initiatives and a raft of 'earth-friendly' organisations – all drawing attention to **'green' issues**. Paradoxically, the internet –

a high-tech communicative medium – has strengthened and connected these assemblies, bringing them and some of their more 'low tech' aims to the public's attention. There are encouraging signs of change – the environmental debate has made clear the need to stop unsustainable building practices, such as housing with high energy demands, as well as the fact that our housing development is inextricably linked to a **greater whole**.

respect for the land

' We are part of this whole – we are not the whole. Our being here is really the most transitory aspect of the planet. It is trees, it is climate, it is the earth, the water, the rocks and the landscape which are real. When we fail to see ourselves belonging to and as a part of that we become unreal. ' [2]

Pritzker prize-winning architect Glenn Murcutt's holistic approach to his architectural trade is embraced by a growing number of practitioners in the design and construction industry. If we believe, as they do, that our lives and actions on this living planet are **interconnected**, then respect for the land, and caring for the earth and its beings, becomes the **foundation for living**. Whatever we put into the earth will come back to us in some form. Dangerous building practices in the past are now surfacing as today's health problems. Housing relying on technology has contributed to **global warming**, acid rain and toxicity to land and sea.

In the early 1960s a whole generation was alerted to these **warning signs** by Rachel Carson in her book *Silent Spring*. The 1970s oil crisis drew attention to the long-term viability of fossil fuels – oil, coal and gas – while the effect of the continued use of these **finite resources** manifested itself during the 1980s in global warming caused by greenhouse gas emissions. Buildings accounted for around 50 per cent of emissions created by humans. In Australia alone it is estimated that households produce 105 million tonnes of greenhouse gas per annum – an average of 15 tonnes of **greenhouse gas** per home each year.[3] Think of that as our air-conditioning units hum away.

In the 1990s no one could fail to have been affected in some way by freak weather patterns, **disruptive** climate changes and pollution to the soil and our oceans. Anyone still doubting the impact of houses and life in the industrialised countries should read the 1995 report *A Building Revolution*. It revealed that 40 per cent of the world's materials and energy are used by buildings, 30 per cent of new or renovated buildings suffer from 'sick building syndrome' and 55 per cent of the timber felled for non-fuel uses is for construction.[4]

On an optimistic note the report observes that 'as severe as these problems are, combinations of **ancient techniques** and available technologies can eliminate almost all the damage new buildings do – making buildings healthy and reducing utility bills dramatically. As an even larger bonus, they create homes and workplaces that are more desirable to live in and more productive to work in. And the high home values and productive offices resulting from "ecological design" are capturing the attention of real-estate developers and investors'.[5]

envisage a future

There are many positive indications that environmentally sustainable development is becoming seen as imperative for humankind's survival. Many governments and councils are introducing accreditation systems for the construction industry and implementing **environmental** building codes for new houses and apartments. Elements of these systems include energy performance estimations, cross-ventilation, access to solar power, areas of 'soft soil' as opposed to concrete, worm farms and composting facilities. It is possible to imagine a future in which every new building will have to comply with a range of ecological measures – encompassing everything from the materials it is made from to estimations for its ongoing energy consumption.

A checklist based on commonsense – equating to a sound ecological rationale – might well include guidelines such as the following. Buildings, preferably smaller ones, should be founded on the principles and practices of **minimal impact** and sustainability. They need to be appropriately sited, be non-polluting, use 'planet friendly' materials, employ waste-reduction systems and work with the local environment. Proposals should meet the aesthetic objectives of a rural or city scape. Dwellings should be **energy efficient** and low maintenance. Furnishings, on whatever scale, should begin with materials that will meet our health requirements and ensure the **conservation of the future**.

minute gestures

Actions such as stopping junk mail, **choosing** to use non-toxic paints, saving power and composting scraps can be instigators of a broader awareness of how we live. Approaching the **minutiae of living** with a green sensibility can also help us question our perceptions of what constitutes good and aesthetically pleasing architecture – homely appearances can sometimes be deceptive.

material choice

At first glance a number of alternative building methods might seem radical, extreme or simply primitive. But closer examination of these alternatives shows that many do have a unique aesthetic appeal and, most importantly, are **low in embodied energy** – the amount of energy needed to create a product. This has **significant implications** when we consider undertaking any building or renovation project. For example, earth and aggregates are extremely low in embodied energy, whereas glass, plastic, copper and aluminium are high and involve a variety of processes including transport, heat applications and mining in their making. A building can be classified in terms of its embodied energy – a consideration of the amount of energy consumed by all the processes in its production. A dwelling built with **reused and salvaged materials** or one of hand-puddled mud bricks would be considered very low in embodied energy; one incorporating kiln-fired bricks, steel and plate glass would be significantly higher in embodied energy and would have a correspondingly greater environmental impact. In **evaluating** our **material** choice we should also remember that a number of natural resources are finite – for instance, it is estimated that supplies of aluminium ore will run out before 2020. Many materials, including aluminium, can be recycled, although this adds to their embodied energy – **reusing** is the preferred option. As a rule of thumb, materials requiring a lot of processing are more costly to the environment than those requiring less.

In some cases there might be justification for using materials and methods high in embodied energy – for instance, if they provide a lasting, low-maintenance building and can **significantly reduce** the operational energy consumed during its lifetime.

And on longevity, the life of an average home in the USA is about 35 years; in Australia, New Zealand and Britain, around 55 years.[6] Therefore it is particularly important to construct with **durability** in mind – to avoid drawing on more resources – and to design **adaptable** buildings that can accommodate changes in use over centuries.

So, when it comes to choosing materials and construction methods, we should ask: what is low in embodied energy, can be sourced close to the site, is **appropriate** for the site, might **reduce impact** on the environment and is good for our health? Consider alternatives outside of conventional construction and follow David Suzuki's suggestion of looking to nature:

'*Industries that are designing means of production can follow the example of nature in which one species' waste is another's opportunity ... material is used, transformed and used again in a never-ending cycle. We can transform our thinking from the linearity of extracting, processing, manufacturing, selling, using and discarding into the circularity of natural cycles.*' [7]

If we can adopt **sustainable** living and appreciate the beauty inherent in **raw and unusual materials**, an earth-friendly visual lexicon can emerge from our own devising, from what we feel is right and wrong, from what we consider to be ugly or beautiful. Perhaps, given more space on the cover, the title of this book might well have included *Bamboo*, *Bottles*, *Cardboard*, *Bundled Reeds*, *Hemp*, *Car Parts* and *Panels,* all manner of discarded and recycled *Scrap* and *Fabrics,* as well as *Sticks*, *Stones* and *Mud*. With ingenuity, determination and a **twist** in aesthetic sensibility, unconventional materials can often be **adapted** to be used in dwellings in some way. Salvaged items can be combined with sound contemporary building products low in **embodied energy** to create wonderfully individual spaces that redefine the conventions of home-building.

natural elements

This resourceful, 'back to basics' **studio retreat** is set on a wooded slope with distant ocean views and blends easily into its surroundings. The materials used in construction have come from the land that it stands lightly upon – **sticks, stone, mud** and pieces salvaged from the property's original dilapidated outbuildings. Its rugged charm recalls early pioneer houses and the improvisation of rural barns and sheds – beauty from essential function and an economic combination of materials.

The owner and builder is a potter – a passionate devotee of the art of wood-fired ceramics, and also of the surrounding native bushland. He explains that the house is 'accidentally' sited just below the ridge line on a level originally marked for vegetable growing: 'The four posts that went in for the garden shed seemed to dictate what followed. I found some rabbit-proof wire netting, sprang it between the upright poles and added clay to either side, building it up much like a pot. This was then coated with a layer of cow dung. I liked the process and just carried on building'.

With the workshop built and the issue of somewhere to sleep resolved, the main living structure, with its welcoming hearth, came together over three years of weekend building, one side remaining open to the elements. The owner says, 'The steep slope influenced the construction and the natural drainage lines dictated where the workshop should go'. The workshop, several strides from the house, occupies the site of the former vegetable garden, which is now 'up top' and corralled against marauding wildlife. The location has a cool-temperate climate: 'You might suffer a cold snap for a day or two and then it comes good again. The temperature might get down to 14 on a bad day. On a wintry day you just put on another jumper and a beanie'.

Outward appearances reflect an honest approach in design together with a commonsensical, practical nature.

The **'open to the elements'** dry composting toilet and invigorating outdoor shower share magnificent country views, but this pared-down approach to living might not suit those needing creature comforts. The ambience, however, has a wonderfully restorative effect. On one particular visit, enjoying the evening breeze through the open corner room, the owner served tea from a hand-thrown pot and cups, bringing to mind a passage written by Christopher Day:

' It is necessary to cultivate a sense for beauty, for the artistic. I say "necessary" because our culture tends to suppress this sense, and "cultivate" because everyone has it latent within them. It used to be so strong that pre-industrial common people could not make a spoon, a cart, a boat, even a house look ugly ... all they made and did was essentially functional; there was no time, energy or space to make anything without a practical purpose; beauty and utility were inseparable. ' [8]

Surely Cezanne and Van Gogh would have enjoyed an opportunity to paint this rugged still life. The owner recalls, 'The first thing I built was this table, something to put my pots on'.

Home is where the hearth is. The paving surround is made up of bricks, under-fired from a local supplier. The chimney is made out of dirt and broken stones, rather than mud bricks. The hot-water tank (not shown) sits by the fire and is connected to the header tank to supply hot water to the shower.

above: Looking back at the open-corner living room and 'back door'; the floor is raised above ground-level to 'discourage death adders'. All stone used in the building came from the site, with sand and cement used in only one section.

right: The poles for the workshop are sunk a metre into the ground. According to the owner–builder, 'If you want to do it properly, you actually burn the end section that goes into the ground, charring it – this gives protection against termites. Notice any well-burnt log in the bush: the termites won't touch it – they don't like the carbon – and the firing also takes out any excess moisture from the log'.

facing page: A visiting potter's cups await completion alongside a traditional Leach kick wheel: 'I sometimes have other potters come to spend time here – I like the exchange'.

above top: The workshop is elevated to provide workspace underneath. The owner plans to add a 'skirt' around it to stop the rain blowing into the workspace.

above: The shower – 'I collect more water than I need from the roofs', says the owner, 'and the soil here is really good material for puddled bricks. The wall in the shower is standing up really well'.

left: The owner getting all fired up with the kiln, his favourite toy: 'I like the idea of my firings as creative play tied to life's rhythms'. The firing process takes a month.

nostalgia for mud

We have an instinctive response to the soil from an early age – who, as a child, has managed to resist the urge to make mud pies or sit happily trickling earth through tiny fingers? The French have a saying, *nostalgie de la boue* – nostalgia for mud – a phrase that can be more loosely translated to mean 'having a longing to get back to one's roots'. It seems an apt way to remind ourselves of both our formative beginnings and the fact that earth – **the source of life** – was also the provider of our earliest shelters.

We can trace former human occupation back to the earth-dug caves of Vallonet in France some 900,000 years ago. Our troglodyte ancestors had good reason to go underground – digging into earth or soft rock for protection has many advantages, not least the stabilising effect it has on temperature. Today many people continue to live successfully under the earth's surface, including an estimated 40 million people in China. There are cities carved into the rocks of Cappadocia in Turkey, cliff dwellings in France and inhabited caves in Tunisia and Spain. A community of opal miners lives underground in Coober Pedy in Australia, and in Kansas City in the USA old limestone mines have been converted for various commercial purposes.

The **history** of earthen architecture is, though, in a word, buried, literally, in the past and in contemporary documentation. Technological developments in housing have alienated us from the ground, with our reliance on the perceived benefits of a 'machine age' leading to belief that earth is a dirty word, best not used in reference to architecture. This ill-informed approach denies the fact that earth buildings have all the qualities that we look for in sustainable dwellings. The use of earth can be linked to Mesopotamia 5000 years ago and there are cities of 'clay' over 2000 years old in Yemen and Iran. The Spaniards took mud techniques to South America, bringing about the adobe buildings of Taos and Santa Fe. And, if some remain hesitant about the validity of mud as a construction material, consider that around 40 per cent of the world's population lives in mud dwellings.

Earth remains the dominant building material in parts of Central and South America, Africa, Asia and India – some climates and countries being more suited to its use than others. Valued for being widely available and often on-site, earth requires little processing, can be very durable and has **good thermal mass** – that is, the ability to absorb and release heat, thus moderating fluctuations in temperature. The use of earth in structures reduces our reliance on timber and other conventional materials that might be high in embodied energy. Ironically, in countries where earth was once an indispensable vernacular, governments now consider it inferior to introduced, inappropriate building materials and technology, while in the outer city limits of many industrialised societies, earth-building is rapidly acquiring status and being legislated. Contemporary buildings made from earthen materials in Australia, Europe and the USA constitute a **growing** field, and why not? These are construction methods proven over thousands of years and now adapted successfully for contemporary living.

earth forms

The appearance of granular-textured, hand-shaped surfaces caught in the glancing rays of warm evening light has an **allure** that strikes to the core of our being. The combination of thickset walls with a tactile rounded finish, offset by the angular, rough timber frames of windows and doors, is a marriage of primitive materials. The construction process is personally involving, empowering the builder with creativity – birthing the **organic** earthen forms to life. Methods might be hand-labour intensive but that can be **positive**, bringing people together for building and annual repairs – a time for unity and renewing connection to the land. It is said that living in a house fashioned in this way creates a feeling of **harmony** and a sense of being well-grounded. There is much to gain from the traditions of earthen construction – how we might **'return to earth'**.

left and middle insets: The monumentally buttressed adobe churches of New Mexico have captivated many artists and photographers, including Georgia O'Keefe and Ansel Adams.

right inset: The natural forms of El Santuario De Chimayo – the 'El Lourdes' of New Mexico for those who believe its 'sacred earth' has the power to heal.

left: The strong earthen forms of the Museum of Fine Arts in Santa Fe, a fine example of Pueblo revival architecture. In many types of mud architecture the timber framing remains as scaffolding when the mud coating needs renewing.

above: Hand-puddled bricks used to build the Barlows'
house, featured on the following pages. There are many
scientific methods for testing if soil is suitable for mud
bricks, but this builder chose a more primitive test: the
'drop test', where a brick is lifted to waist-height and
dropped on the ground; if it breaks, the soil mix fails
and another mix is trialled.

right: Machine-compressed mud bricks with a compressing
machine and earth mixer. They have smoother lines and
can be immediately stacked to dry, whereas hand-puddled
mud bricks require a sunny spell of weather or a covered
area set aside in order for hardening to take place.

1 mud slinging

'The humble mud brick alone could be the one catalyst to stimulate cooperative living instead of competitive destruction.'
Alistair Knox [9]

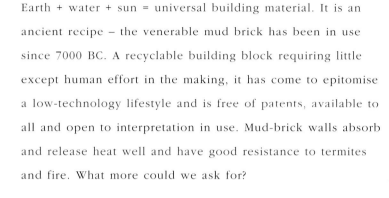

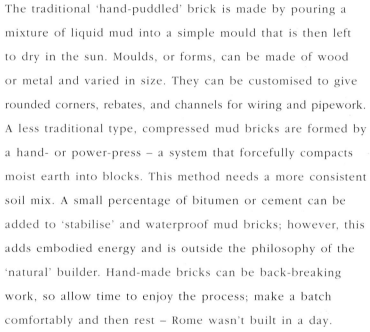

Earth + water + sun = universal building material. It is an ancient recipe – the venerable mud brick has been in use since 7000 BC. A recyclable building block requiring little except human effort in the making, it has come to epitomise a low-technology lifestyle and is free of patents, available to all and open to interpretation in use. Mud-brick walls absorb and release heat well and have good resistance to termites and fire. What more could we ask for?

The traditional 'hand-puddled' brick is made by pouring a mixture of liquid mud into a simple mould that is then left to dry in the sun. Moulds, or forms, can be made of wood or metal and varied in size. They can be customised to give rounded corners, rebates, and channels for wiring and pipework. A less traditional type, compressed mud bricks are formed by a hand- or power-press – a system that forcefully compacts moist earth into blocks. This method needs a more consistent soil mix. A small percentage of bitumen or cement can be added to 'stabilise' and waterproof mud bricks; however, this adds embodied energy and is outside the philosophy of the 'natural' builder. Hand-made bricks can be back-breaking work, so allow time to enjoy the process; make a batch comfortably and then rest – Rome wasn't built in a day.

Mud bricks can be load-bearing or used as infill, usually between supporting timber posts. In wet climates the prudent builder will design or construct with eaves and footings to protect the earth walls from driving rain, rising moisture and flooding. Building follows the conventions of kiln-fired bricklaying. A mud mortar is used for bonding, although bricks will simply stick together if they have been quickly soaked in water. When complete, walls can be left in their natural state or rendered in a variety of materials, including coats of emulsifying cow dung and mud. Timeless adobe structures – aesthetically pleasing and therapeutic to live in – are thus fashioned from the land and its living creatures.

return to
Earth

the Barlows' mud-brick home

Reaching this mud-brick house, hidden deep in a coastal forest, requires patient negotiation of a wending dirt trail through dense woodland, the rough journey only increasing visitors' anticipation and introducing them to the beautiful land.

First impressions leave an indelible sense of place. The house melds with its surroundings, its form suggesting that resourceful bush-Australia met and embraced the New Mexico building vernacular. Structure arises from a natural association of building materials: reclaimed bridge supports, local timbers and hand-puddled mud bricks made from the ground they stand on. A feeling of security is given to the house and garden by the presence of a perimeter wall, utility buildings and a screened vegetable patch. Entrance to this enclave is through a metalworked gate, which adds a sculptural flourish to the shaded pergola walkway. Self-sufficiency and respect for the land are worn prominently on the sleeve – biodegradable construction materials, roof-mounted solar panels, a bountiful kitchen garden and a dam, with water-wise plantings completing the scene.

The owners, garden designer Robyn Barlow and her husband, Julian, once a builder and now a Feldenkrais practitioner, made the 'sea change' to this idyllic spot with their two sons after years of Melbourne inner-city living. As a builder, Julian had worked with a number of major architects, absorbing influences and accumulating salvage – 'three or four semi-trailer loads' – to build this, their fifth family home.

'The whole approach is truth in materials and proportions ... wrought iron can create a whole new aesthetic dimension when used with earth walls.' Alistair Knox on environmental building. His son Aliatair made the gate.

An architect, Wendy Nettle, helped the duo articulate their plans for a 'simple house' using a grid system based on the proportions of their collected furnishings, including doors, windows and the old bridge beams.

The couple chose cement-rendered mud-brick walls for 'versatility and protection from any hard-driving rain'. Julian says, 'The medium suits my style of building. I like rounded corners and wanted more control over the insets for doors and windows – with mud brick you're able to change things as you go', adding, 'The walls are very "touchable", they give atmosphere, a romantic ambience, one that you don't normally get with other hard surfaces'. Julian hand-made the mud bricks, using custom-made metal frames (see photograph, page 36), and found that, when building with mud bricks, 'You have to be involved, the brick itself doesn't allow you to be detached from the building'.

The construction of the house allowed for an intuitive integration of existing materials. Julian elaborates: 'No matter how stringent the design, you have to be flexible – and it's a great way to build when you allow the materials to tell you what to do. It's just a matter of being open enough; the materials can tell you where they want to be organised and fit into the house. It sounds crazy but it works'.

There's certainly a feeling of wellbeing in the house. The ground floor is given over to laidback living, a pleasing 'flow' resulting from the light-filled open layout. Music and the smell of baking bread waft through the air, further unifying the rooms. There's easy access to integral outdoor spaces on both sides of the house, with the enclosed central lawn a secure play area for the boys in earlier days. The potted fruit trees and Robyn's edible plantings offer sustenance and attractive displays throughout the year.

This holistic approach to home-making resonates with the philosophies of Alistair Knox,[10] a pioneer of earth-building in Australia after World War II and with whom Julian once worked. A man with admirable if somewhat idealistic principles, Knox might not have accommodated the use of a cement render on the mud bricks, preferring 'cow dung mixed 50–50 with a binding of top soil'. In fairness to Julian, a man not averse to experimenting with building materials, he did try this but 'The smell caused me to hallucinate badly!'

The Barlows speak with passion about living and building, a philosophic attitude infusing their work. They suggest the thought processes that go into making a home are as important as the constituent parts, saying, 'A building should be respectful to the materials and, if you are honest about being respectful and your intention is honourable, you'll get a building with a lot more integrity, and it's that integrity people respond to'. Clearly there's a sound ethos, aesthetic harmony and soulful approach at work here. The couple have drawn on their collective skills and imagination to create a very special home, a place that invites attachment and invokes a warm response from family and friends.

facing page: Gaps in the wooded surrounds of the approach road allow glimpses of the meandering river estuary, a natural boundary on three sides of the property.

right: 'We chose the house site down from the ridge for shelter and to be close to the river', explains Robyn. 'There is a nice swimming hole as well as access for the boat; the boys used to take the tinny as a short-cut to the school bus.'

below: Timber framework punctuates the solar shed used to store batteries.

above: A utilitarian mix of materials and finishes: nearly all the fittings were salvaged by Julian from a 1950s kitchen in Melbourne.

left: Daily life for the family starts in the kitchen, sited to benefit from the early-morning sun. It's a space that invites communal cooking and conversation. Says Robyn, 'We have friends visiting from Melbourne who arrive with boxes of food and love going out to the vegetable garden. We can all cook together – I like that'. The grand-scale window lets in natural light and bush views.

above: In winter temperatures drop to minus 4 degrees Celsius and solar power can be limited. To overcome this the Barlows have an old-fashioned slow-combustion wood stove, which uses fallen timber from the property as fuel. This boosts power, supplying hot water for showers and radiant heaters.

facing page: The twin living area, housing a billiard room, small office and an expansive lounge, is divided by a massive fireplace framed by recycled iron-bark bridge posts and the exposed mud-brick structure – the owners playing with finished and unfinished looks. Julian's 'Brancusi inspired' angular rough-hewn stools stand alongside comfy sofas on the mountain ash floorboards. Lights are operated using pull cords to avoid switches marring natural wall surfaces.

above: An open staircase of sawn logs and customised metalwork strides through a generous area that combines upper-level access with the library, desk space and coat storage. Old bridge timbers are supports for the upper floor and visibly jut across the timber-panelled ceiling.

right: Alistair Knox would have surely approved of this well-proportioned dining area. He believed that 'well-pierced mud walls can show the thickness of the walls and add architectural punctuation' and recommended employing 'heavy adzed lintels over doorways and weight-bearing arches. Nothing gives a greater sense of wellbeing'.

above: The main bedroom is sited above the kitchen to benefit from rising warmth in winter months. There are wonderful treetop views from the small deck.

facing page: In the tiny downstairs washroom a salvaged window gives an intense slice of forest views. There's a strange but appropriate 'nesting' quality to the mud infill around the handbasin – who could resist scratching their initials in it?

above left: Hens and roosters forage around the *Cordyline australis* (cabbage tree) and fruit trees.

below left: Close to the house Robyn chose water-wise plantings – echiums and cordylines – together with hardy native grasses, all planned to withstand a local climate with poor rainfall. Past the salvaged gate is Julian's workshed.

above right: On summer days outdoor areas function as extended living spaces. The house is also sited to maximise passive solar power in winter. The pergola is draped in wisteria and a deciduous grapevine, which provide shade on hot summer days but, in cold months, lose their leaves, allowing in the warming winter sun.

below right: The house runs on solar power: 'We now have 20 solar panels – the energy goes into a battery bank. It's worked beautifully; we've had no power bills for eight years. The initial outlay was about the same as bringing the grid out with unsightly poles'.

Natural manures are used in the kitchen garden to provide seasonal vegetables and fruits. With tempting provender on display, total enclosure was necessary to, as Robyn says, 'prevent marauding wallabies, bowerbirds and parrots. Those two birds are enough to devour the entire vegetable garden – they are very cheeky'.

above: A salvaged grid gate provides a safe keep for the hens and roosters at night.

right and facing page: Robyn's garden is a sensory experience: there is beauty in the folds of a common cabbage and the spiky demeanour of an artichoke.

mud

mud

glorious

an artist's mud-brick house

Pristine bushland is the setting for this picturesque mud-brick and stone property, one of five dwellings sited unobtrusively on 25 acres set aside for a small colony of artists. The studio home bears the signature palette of its owner on a textural exterior wall, the ochre-coloured mass needing but a few vertical poles and a simple kitchen window to complete a natural composition. The other side of the wall holds a moulded niche and an integral wine rack fabricated from terracotta pipes – the naive 'cow' assemblage complementing the spirit of improvisation.

What is it about an artist's workplace that stirs the imagination?
Is it the tangible air of 'possibility' that hovers over an array
of wet paint and jars stuffed with brushes – materials ready
at hand to help express visual intuition and thought?

Or can we point to more specific items that seem to radiate
creative 'potential' – unusual artefacts, offbeat cards and old
posters pinned to paint-spattered walls?

And why is it that artists and designers seem to have a 'way'
with furnishings? Assortments of oddball tables and chairs
from the plain and practical to the strangely ornate effortlessly
acquire cohesion – falling compatibly into their household
place. Sometimes these arty environments begin to encourage

us to view corners of rooms, flowers and eclectic arrangements as realisable still lifes.

Owner and artist, Elisabeth Cummings used to live in the city but always hankered after a studio in the countryside, the Australian landscape inspiring many of her sought-after pieces. 'There's something about the calligraphy of the bush that I find endlessly fascinating. It's a very mutable thing, always shifting and full of ambiguity', says Elisabeth, who initially painted out of an old army tent on the site.

Over time, invigorated by the location, she decided to erect something more permanent, drawing on materials from the land and setting the building right at the edge of the bush. Talking about the process, Elisabeth says, 'Pip Giovanelli was the main builder, he did the excellent stone foundations. Later Clark Walton worked with him, and there were many other helpers who came and went'. Giovanelli recalls, 'There was little disturbance to the area, the few cleared trees were put to good use as posts and interior support, branches used for bracing. Building was very much an organic process; the majority of bricks were made using a hand-puddled method, with sand-rich clay and straw, and a metal frame about 9 by 18 inches. They were pretty heavy – a lot cracked. Liz had made some other bricks using a Cinva press, so we laid those as well as the broken halves using a mud mortar. There was also a wattle and daub section'.

The use of the shell as a motif in Italian Renaissance art inspired Elisabeth to make a window: 'I just cut into the mud-brick wall, fashioning the shell like a piece of sculpture with "ribs" of clay'. The glorious mud finish was achieved with a lot of slurry. Says Giovanelli, 'We'd work it into the rough surface with vulcanised rubbergloves – a very satisfying way of finishing it all off. On completion the house looked as if it had been there for all time'.

Living so close to the bush, though, can have its drawbacks. Elisabeth recalls, 'One bushfire in 1994 destroyed a small studio but the house and contents survived'. The original building has since been sympathetically extended by her architect son using corrugated iron to add a round cornered bedroom/living space, the additional roof better supplying all the house water. During winter Elisabeth finds that the softer light 'creates wonderful shadows and I'll still paint inside and out. I don't want to be closed in and just wear a lot of clothes to combat the chill – sometimes the fingers and toes do go numb! When it gets too cold at night I'll light a fire'.

2 terra firma

the techniques of rammed earth

Devotees of rammed earth, like their sister adobe-advocates, love to spread the word on earthly matters. And with good reason: this is another ancient, environmentally friendly building method with which to create beautiful and enduring walls.

In Turkistan, remains of buildings made from blocks of rammed earth date back to around 8000 BC and in Assyria to 4000 BC.

Today's earth-builders are keen to remind us that original sections of the Great Wall of China were rammed in 700 BC and still stand. In the mid-sixteenth century the technique spread through Europe. Many rammed earth buildings remain in Germany, England and France, where the technique is referred to as *pisé de terre* – the word *pisé* is commonly used today.

In recent centuries the method surfaced periodically when conventional building supplies were low or unavailable – for example, during the 1930s Depression in the USA and earlier in Australia during colonisation. Since the 1970s the rammed earth method has, like mud brick, experienced a revival through the 'back to the land' movement and the increasing interest in sustainable lifestyles.

So, with the main ingredient widely available, is it all 'easy pisé'? Not exactly – the process has many benefits but intensive labour is required. Traditionally the technique involved using a hand-held pole to manually bed the earth mixture in between wooden box forms. Today builders are more likely to use mechanical earth-movers to ease the loading and pneumatic tampers to compress the soil in reusable, recycled plastic formwork. To improve durability, strength and moisture resistance, a small percentage of cement is often added to the mix, giving rise to the term 'stabilised rammed earth'.

Building with earth often brings communities together. The Immaculate Heart of Mary, a parish development at Thurgoona, Australia, drew on the resources and skills of the resident priests, parishioners and specialist builders during design and construction. The church foyer (above top) features recycled spotted-gum timber. Inside, the magnificent roof trusses and their original bolts enjoy new life after salvation from the wreckage of a former hospital circa 1935. The church's richly coloured walls support arched sandblasted concrete lintels (above).

The finished stratified look can be varied in texture according to both the way the soil is rammed and its aggregate content. A sandy mix, for example, gives a finer, smooth result – the markings left by the forms adding interest. The thick 'clean limbed' appearance of rammed earth walls appeals to residential and commercial users. The latter includes many trades wanting to emphasise their 'earth' connections: look out for vineyard buildings, four-wheel drive showrooms, and community and tourist centres in country locations.

Aesthetically impressive and with 'dirt cheap' ingredients, rammed earth also has other advantages.

▼ It is relatively simple to source and construct, and therefore has low embodied energy.

▼ Dwellings can be built by owner-builders, as many informative websites testify.

▼ Rammed walls have compressive strength – stabilised earth in particular can be load-bearing up to many storeys.

▼ Built naturally, walls are non-toxic, can 'breathe' and are acoustically sound.

▼ Rammed walls are low maintenance and have an intrinsic finish: they require no additional coats of plaster or paint.

▼ Walls have good resistance to termites, fire and earthquakes.

▼ Earth for building can be found on or close to site – a building's appearance then blends with its locale.

▼ Rammed earth walls have good thermal mass – that is, they absorb heat and cold, releasing them slowly to maintain a comfortable environment – benefiting passive solar strategies and potentially lowering operating costs.

above left: Work in progress on a very singular rammed earth house. Note the unusually shaped recesses on the completed sections. Walls are typically around 600 millimetres thick and use 45-degree-angle corners to minimise wear and tear.

middle left: Prior to ramming, tests can be done to assess soil suitability and colour. Additives to improve water-resistance can also be trialled. These samples were formed in pipes and labelled to identify.

below left: Rammed earth lends itself to various forms of imprints, embossing, insets and apertures (see the leaf on page 64). Apertures might require custom-made forms as in these triangular windows at Charles Sturt University.

facing page: An old barn wall, rammed naturally without additives, wears its age well. The builder calls this a 'wall with wrinkles', contending that many people 'prefer their homes to emulate fashion, young forever'. He recommends that his clients 'let the years add a bit of character'.

a sustainable design

Set in a harsh landscape previously degraded by land clearing and farming, the award-winning Charles Sturt University campus at Thurgoona, Australia, sets out to actively demonstrate how environmentally responsible architecture and sustainable living can be achieved. It combines a prominent use of rammed earth walls with the modern technologies of solar heating and environmental control using computers. Low-energy strategies include the use of thermal mass, building orientation and distinctive thermal chimneys. Naturally the site is landscaped to retain a healthy native ecosystem. Ensuring that these strategies were noticeable was part of the challenge that the project architect, Marci Webster-Mannison, set herself: 'Making the philosophy highly visible was deliberate because one of the objectives of sustainable design is to change how people think and live, and how we use things'.

The hot, dry summer climate of the Thurgoona region means that the harvesting and storage of rainwater is critical. The 52 steel water-tanks are neatly incorporated into the structure and add to the thermal mass; the two shown stand like sentinels, linking the huge, curving span of a rammed earth wall. Their prominence acts as a visible reminder to conserve resources. The campus-devised water-management system has won three state government awards.

Organic matters

new angles for compact living

This unconventional retreat is
dynamically shaped to fit the land
and trees with minimal effect on
nature. Anchored at the rear by three
complementary-sized rammed earth
walls, the rest of the house pans out
to a view of a small wooded valley.

When Judy Isaacs started looking for a spot to dwell she found herself gravitating back to Eltham, an attractive bush suburb of Melbourne where she had lived on previous occasions. The area is popular with those seeking a change of lifestyle and is considered the centre of earth-building in Australia. Painter Justus Jörgensen had established the artistic community of Montsalvat with a *pisé de terre* building in 1934.

Studios and 'farm' buildings for food production followed during World War II, a European-style village arising from an imaginative use of local earth, stone and timbers together with items salvaged from wreckers' yards. After the war inspirational 'earth' architect Alistair Knox lit a torch for owner-builders to follow, motivating many in Eltham and far beyond to build with mud-brick — his influence remains strong today.

left: For the architect, 'The building dances with the trees and contours ... there's a sense of poise in movement about the house'. The vertical cladding of yellow stringy bark has a distinctive pattern resulting from the irregular plank widths and cutting angles of radial sawing.

below: The custom-made deck rails were inspired by the criss-crossing of the tree branches that surround the creek. The motif is echoed in timber on the internal stair rail and bedroom balustrade.

Alternative building continues to thrive in the region, an appropriate locale for this quirky residence. The house is curiously shaped so as to fit around existing trees and the lie of the land, turning its back on a bordering dual carriageway and orientating out to capture the sun and panoramic views of the valley, home to many wild creatures such as frogs, wallabies and wombats.

The plot immediately attracted Judy, who visualised the potential lying beneath the engulfing thickets of wild blackberry bushes. A keen permaculture gardener, Judy says she felt bound to 'acquire the knowledge of the land and know how to use it', and weeks spent clearing the brambles made her familiar with the local climate and the site's nature. The choice of architect Greg Burgess was apt; he is renowned for creating houses with an 'organic footprint' and is responsible for several community buildings in the Eltham area.

'The development process was a delight', Judy recalls. 'It was good to have someone responding to and observing the land as I had been doing, feeling the winds, the path of the sun, regarding the trees and the way water ran into the valley.' Greg Burgess remembers that the brief was a 'good one, Judy had aspirations for the small home to be as low impact and as sustainable as possible'.

Both knew, though, that the site was awkward, being, as Greg describes, 'a challenging triangle, restricted between the busy road on its high embankment to one side and the lovely creek to the fore'. The problem of traffic noise was solved by the strategic placement of the stabilised earth walls. The generous porch is defined by two of the earth walls, the main one providing a naturally textured backdrop to the living area and the bedroom above, the smaller shaping the kitchen to the right of the entrance. The earth walls function as structural insulation as well as sound insulation, with their geometry and compacted form also appealing to the eye. Skylight windows slowly twist from the incline of the rear wall to vertical – one of many unusual complexities about the structure.

Judy recalls Greg often referring to the place as 'a hardworking house', every nook and alcove created for a purpose. There is a study/guest room tucked away at the rear behind the third rammed wall and space was also found on the ground floor for a bathroom with a dry composting toilet. The first floor is cut diagonally away from the full-height windows next to the main deck, allowing an effective light well.

Greg talks about 'a dynamic relationship of the spaces in the home, both vertically and horizontally', and the interior has certainly been given a lively feel. There's an intriguing play of angles both in the floor plan and the detailing, but the whole is underpinned by an 'organic' logic, the house unfolding naturally to the views and light. Getting a balance with the land was important for Judy, but she also feels that 'the home-building process was also an opportunity to discover something about myself. It was a commitment, a statement of intent and an expression of my philosophy'.

above right: Rainwater is collected from the gently sloping roof into a large vertical tank. The eaves extend generously to shelter the top corner bedroom deck, which emerges from the site, 'floating' out over the creek.

middle right: Unusual angles and immaculate detailing continue in the kitchen, where all the action takes place around a uniquely shaped centre bench with a top of recycled red gum. The cupboard fronts are Tasmanian maple and their interiors are made from boards of compressed rice hulls; the unusually panelled ceilings are hoop pine plywood.

below right: In the living area light from the southern skylights falls softly across the back wall, a surface textured by the formwork that originally contained it. The stairs are partly made from recycled red gum.

facing page: Comfy chairs, set around an efficient wood fire, which uses fallen logs only, is the perfect winter scene. In warmer weather sliding doors give access to the deck; the louvred windows provide ventilation.

bramare
a greenprint for a calming refuge

A tranquil pastoral valley overlooked by a forested hillside is the peaceful setting for this contemporary rammed earth structure.

It is a comfortable and expansive home, the light-filled kitchen and living area busy on this occasion with the laughter and spirited chat of the owner's six nieces. Andrew Barling, enjoying their company after a spell of hard work, confides, 'It's good to be home. This place has a quality I never tire of. Visitors also relax as soon as they step in, and the aspect from the bedrooms is glorious'.

Andrew and his wife, Judy Burley, looked to settle back in

Australia after a trip to Italy and enjoyed many country excursions before finding 'the property that we had always dreamt of' in the environs of Bendigo, Victoria. They called the place 'Bramare', meaning 'to yearn for' – an appropriate epithet given the beautiful locale.

An environmentally sensitive house was top of the couple's building agenda and Andrew recalls that 'Judy had seen some "red dirt" rammed earth houses in central Australia and liked the sense of connection they gave to the land'. They admired architect Dennis Carter's previous work with rammed earth, and Judy, who was fully involved in the design and

construction phase, gave the architect their brief for 'an energy-efficient home that would capture the views, provide informal living and have enough room for extended family visits'.

The local climate in this part of Victoria is a harsh one. Long, scorching summers follow bitterly cold winters, extremes that Dennis is both familiar with and designs for. Passive cooling principles are incorporated into the building's 'smart' orientation and layout. Wide eaves angled to the sky shield in summer but allow a lower winter sun to penetrate the interior; polished concrete floors store the heat. The architect elegantly combined ancient and new technology –

rammed earth walls with solar collectors on the roof and gas-fired hot water coursing through the floors for cold spells. Fans and room dividers with 'gaps' assist cross-ventilation of the air introduced through the many louvred windows. Hoop pine, a plantation-grown timber, is used on the insulated ceilings, which are supported by light steel framing. Drought comes with the territory so all roof water is harvested and stored in three large tanks – all clearly visible, as many of the 'workings' are. An on-site plant processes sewage; grey and waste water is recycled to feed plants at the east end of the house.

Importantly the house feels good to be in – attributable to generous proportions, spaces that connect easily, and abundant light from floor-to-ceiling windows. Detailing throughout is clean and simple, the emphasis on a practical structure and honesty of materials. The house is designed around two intersecting axes. A walkway with slit windows defines one axis, running from a walled kitchen garden and water tanks at the west end past utility rooms and the entrance porch to the bedrooms and bathrooms facing east. On the other axis indoor and outdoor living spaces are orientated north for the sun, while the utility rooms and red-faced garage look south.

Once completed, the house and its natural setting gave 'comfort and relief' to Judy, who was fighting cancer. Andrew relates, 'Jude always felt very fortunate to find the property and privileged to live here for six months. To her it was a healing place – she wanted to share what she felt with other people in a similar situation and decided to create a place where people with breast cancer might enjoy "time out". She called it the Otis Foundation'. (Otis – as in Redding – was Judy's much-loved dog.) A short walk away on land set aside from the property, the Foundation uses Bramare as a blueprint: the same successful design and construction team created two similar rammed earth buildings offering a calming refuge. Andrew continues: 'When Jude died it felt like the baton had been passed on to myself and her family, a responsibility to bring the centre to life'.

Now that Judy's vision is realised and the centre up and running, Andrew vows to complete the native plantings and landscaping around Bramare. Friends wondered whether he might find staying on in the home too painful but he says, 'There's a stamp and remembrance of Jude in the place – I find it very reassuring and comforting to be here'.

The light fantastic in the east–west illuminated walkway. The rammed earth walls bear impressions of the moulds used to shape them – a natural finish. Vertical slit windows intensify light coming in and views out. The small size of all the glazed apertures on the south side reduces heat loss in winter.

above: The kitchen area, full of natural light and ventilation, is a wonderful space to refresh the senses at any time of day. Seen beyond, the 'outdoor' room is screened against insects, and old railway sleepers contain the soil in the kitchen garden. The view expands across fields to the wooded slope.

right: An informal, low-level book-reading area allows views across the width of the house.

facing page: A feature stone-wall encloses the internal fireplace. The architect chose galvanised steel for visible structural support and the pergola, together with aluminium for glazing surrounds: 'It's white-ant country here; timber just gets chomped. Aluminium has low ongoing costs and requires no maintenance. It can also be recycled'. The extended corrugated-iron roof is key to the passive shading principles embodied in the design.

following page: The well-considered entrance bears all the hallmarks of a good arrival and departure space, and the windows allow glimpses of approaching visitors.

3

choosing s t r a w s

Whoever wrote the traditional fable about the three little pigs applied the 'bricks-are-best' values of an industrialised society, conveniently disregarding – perhaps for the sake of a good story – the knowledge that traditional cultures around the globe have successfully used straw and other grasses for 'wolf-proof' dwellings for thousands of years (such is the nature of fiction).

The reed homes of the Samarians have a history dating back over 7000 years and the method of their construction is similar to that used for thousands of years by the Marsh Arabs in Southern Iraq. Bamboo-framed shelters with thatches of straw or leaves are found throughout India, China, Brazil, Peru, Borneo and Japan – the last bearing evidence of prehistoric pit houses made from rammed earth, timber posts and beams and grass thatched roofs. Throughout central and northern Europe straw and reed thatched roofs were appreciated for their insulating qualities in the cold winters. Changes from hand-harvesting techniques during the 1950s reduced the use of straw as thatching, but indigenous societies throughout Africa, Europe and the Middle East continue to use straw and reeds in their often seasonal and temporary shelters.

The technology of compressing straw into bales first appeared in the USA in the late 1800s; the use of straw bales as large building blocks followed shortly after. Pioneers in West Nebraska, finding themselves short of construction materials, were motivated to use baled hay for their houses and community structures.

The method resurged in the USA during the 1970s as part of the counter-culture movement, and today straw bale is a rapidly evolving method of construction with a strong owner–builder following. The straw bale 'community' has the air of a self-supporting international family, collecting and disseminating knowledge for its collective interest. Parties as far afield as Canada, France, Guatemala, Russia, England, Australia and the USA swap information on new construction techniques and building code compliance through books, email and international conventions. The guiding ethos is similar to one that aids the development of any worthy vernacular architecture – a shared responsibility to come up with methods appropriate to place and climate.

Illustrating the benefits of this kind of a 'grass roots' movement, an eco-city development has been created in the Australian city of Adelaide. The Christie Walk project is a community-titled development designed to give a living demonstration of how our cities might be developed with ecological values in mind. The straw bale house pictured (below) shares on-site recycling of stormwater, chlorine-free sewage treatment, community garden spaces and facilities with 13 other dwellings. It is considered to be one of the first straw bale houses anywhere to be built with an inner-city street-front location. Paul Downton, architect and occupier, cites, 'Straw bales are inherently low in embodied energy – 1 tonne of concrete requires over 50 times more energy than straw in its manufacture'. The life span of the buildings is expected to exceed 100 years.

A three-storey timber-framed, non-toxic, solar-powered straw bale townhouse in the Christie Walk project, photographed from the community roof-garden.

Straw polling

Traditionally left-over straw from cereal crops is burnt, polluting the air through the release of carbon dioxide. What better than to put this 'waste' product to good use in affordable housing, substantially reducing greenhouse gas emissions. People talk about the atmosphere of 'good fun' often found on a straw bale site – a tangible spirit of creative unity arising from cooperation, skill sharing and teamwork. In practical terms home-building with straw bales makes sense on many levels.

▼ Cereal crops are widely grown and provide an inexpensive material close to hand.

▼ Straw is a renewable source - crops can be grown in less than a year.

▼ Straw bale houses provide very high thermal insulation and seal out weather extremes; the structures are energy-conserving and energy bills are reduced.

▼ Straw bales provide excellent sound insulation, reducing noise.

▼ The raw material is simple and easy to work with - few specialised tools are required.

▼ Properly coated, straw bales have excellent durability and good resistance to fire and pests.

▼ Thick walls give a comforting appearance and allow the sculpting of niches and feature shelves.

▼ The growing of straw can increase employment in rural areas and revive local housing traditions.

▼ Living in straw bale structures can bring about a sense of wellbeing attributable to non-toxic, biodegradable materials and healthy 'breathable' walls.

▼ Building your own straw bale house can bring about a sense of pride and empowerment because it is a low-cost, satisfying and environmentally sound construction method.

Straw bale building technology has developed rapidly in the last 20 years; many hybrid building systems and techniques have arisen from the variation in materials and building compliance codes across countries.

The original Nebraska style of building was load-bearing, with bale walls supporting a roof and upper floors. Today both load-bearing and infill systems (those with a support framework) are used – even existing structures can have walls 'retro-fitted' with straw bales. During construction the bales need to be kept dry from rain and moisture. If the non-load-bearing method is employed, the bales can be stored under the completed roof structure until required. All constructions benefit from careful orientation to maximise passive solar gains and require some kind of foundation system with moisture and termite barriers.

As an alternative to concrete, there have been successful trials with more unconventional footings such as earth-filled tyres and rubble trenches.

Whether load-bearing or infill, bales are usually stacked like oversized interlocking bricks. Framed apertures for doors and windows need some bales to be split and re-tied. Curved walls, integral seating and modifications during progress are easily accomplished because straw bales are a forgiving medium. Walls are tapped into better alignment and can be trimmed for easier rendering. Bales are then coated with layers of render – often an intrinsic finish in itself – requiring no further coats for protection or decoration. Earthen-based renders, which are lower in embodied energy and allow walls more 'breathability', are preferred by 'natural' builders. When a building is properly protected, its life span is almost indefinite. For a healthier construction, use organic straw where available (and give up smoking during the construction of your straw bale building – remember, loose straw is flammable!).

So far so good – a life-changing, environmentally friendly home made from what is essentially a 'waste' product. The success of this low-technology building method also focuses attention on other waste products, such as paper, card and fabrics, that might be baled and used in similar fashion. Straw bale construction is being used for a wide range of applications including stables, wineries and meditation centres and, as the Christie Walk project illustrates, it is by no means confined to country outposts.

earth and straw
an ancient natural alliance

This hen house was erected during a straw bale workshop run by Frank Thomas of Yesterday, Today, Tomorrow in the permaculture garden at the Northern Sydney Institute of TAFE, Ryde. Bales are usually laid flat and require little, if any, reinforcement. However, here, to better accomplish the tight radius, they were laid on edge and bamboo poles were used to stabilise the walls. High-tensile wires compress the straw bale walls before the roof load is applied. These wires pass under the timber 'bottom plate' – a gap left for this purpose – and are then tightened and fastened with gripples. The muddy patches denote gaps, now stuffed with a mixture of cob (clay and straw) before a three-coat render is applied – the last coat will use lime, which has better rain-resistance than clay. Frank prefers earthen renders, saying, 'Cement render is hard and brittle, allowing limited breathability, trapping some moisture within the bales. It also has much higher embodied energy than clay and lime'.

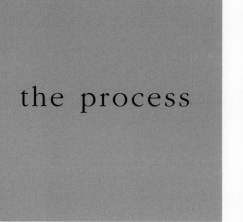

the process

1. A runny mix of clay and water is prepared for the first coat of render.

2. Bales are tapped into better alignment with a mallet before final trimming and rendering.

3. A mixture of cob is prepared; it is about 20 per cent clay and 80 per cent straw, with a dash of lime to help it harden quickly. This mix will fill large gaps in the structure before it is rendered.

4. Cob is used to fill the gaps that often occur where rounded bales meet the straight lines of window and door frames.

5. The cob mix is pushed firmly into the gaps.

6. Straw bale building is a hands-on activity – here, smoothing the cob-filled corners.

7. The first runny coat of render is 'thrown' into the straw, aiming to penetrate the bales as deeply as possible and to provide a key for the next coat.

8. This wall has received its first coat of render; an air gun and compressor were used to forcibly shoot the mix into the bale walls. The custom-made double needle standing on the right is used to re-tie cut bales together. The small sieve ensures the mixture is fine enough.

baLeD UP
in the Blue
MountAins

The striking use of reclaimed
materials in this extraordinary
straw bale house makes the
description 'full of character'
seem inadequate. The home was
built by owners Michael and
Shaina Hennessy and stands on
the site of an old dairy in an
elevated wilderness region.

In winter, when the 'colds' sink to minus 7
degrees Celsius, the place is something of a
cocoon; yet it remains cool in summer when the
mercury hits 40 degrees plus. Straw bale was
an appropriate choice to iron out these climatic
variations, although Shaina says, 'We had initially
thought mud brick, then found we could combine
the two materials. We like the flow of the walls,
and their softness, and I particularly like the
high insulation factor'.

Shaina has a background in design and
renovation and Michael is a carpenter, but
neither had built a place before. They enlisted
Rick Mitchell to help articulate their concepts:
'Two years of caffeine-fuelled jottings on
serviettes'. Shaina recalls, 'We interviewed many
architects but Rick was interested, interesting,
flexible and shared similar beliefs. He expanded
on our ideas and contributed the passive solar
aspect and the permaculture angle'.

The couple set out to create 'a place that would nurture the mind and spirit as well as the body', and it is a stimulating and unique environment, full of imaginative ideas. Michael had collected materials from demolition yards and estimates that '80 per cent of the materials used in the construction were recycled'. These materials included timbers from an old river jetty, 7-metre bush poles from a regrowth area, doors and stained glass windows salvaged from a hospital, and secondhand corrugated iron. Most of the hand-crafted furnishings were made by Michael; other pieces were found at auctions and garage sales.

The house has a number of elements that make it eco-friendly. On the cooler south side of the house, windows are few and small to minimise heat loss in winter and protect from the gale-force winds (see main photograph, previous page). The sleeping and living wings are connected by a central 'tower' with reclaimed leadlight windows (see inset photograph, previous page). The tower functions as a cooling stack in summer when hot air is expelled through the skylights, drawing cool air in from below to maintain temperatures at around 20 degrees Celsius. There's a solar-powered water-heating system on the roof, and the iron walls and ceilings have deep insulation batts.

The building was completed over 18 months and the couple and daughter Scotia enjoyed living in the house. Over a period of seven years they revitalised the whole of the original dairy site, eventually converting the milking shed, a dilapidated workers' cottage and the straw bale house into a mountain retreat to accommodate up to 23 guests. The couple state, 'We will start again on the "perfect" home for ourselves and will definitely use straw bale, mud brick and recycled materials'.

above right: Reclaimed supporting beams are left exposed as a feature in this charming attic bedroom.

middle right: There is nothing standard about the bathrooms. Shaina chose to have old iron fashioned as a surround, and a claw-foot bath re-enamelled to complete the resourceful country look.

below right: The sink was an auction find, and mini-corrugated iron, mud bricks, recycled timbers and straw bales are the combined materials in this small shower room.

facing page: An old-fashioned double entry hall is a traditional ploy to prevent the cold gale-force winds rushing in. The flooring, old convict-made Sandstock bricks pressed into service, harks back to the past. The workings of the tower stairs remain on show, making this area more 'transparent'.

above: The angled return of the window has reassuring depth, a characteristic of straw bale houses. Shaina, inspired by the surrounding nature, 'agonised' over the calming colour scheme in the house.

facing page: A soothing 'still life' composed of textures, finishes and colours. The blistered door was found at a garage sale and left untreated; the cabinet and jug bought at auction.

above: The mud-brick walls on either side of the fireplace absorb the heat of the fire, slowly releasing the accumulated warmth. The unusual canopy over the fireplace was made from a 44-gallon steel drum.

right: The kitchen is fitted out with savvy auction purchases and recycled materials. Michael pieced together the heavy-duty butcher's block, and reclaimed sheet-iron faces the drawers.

facing page: The welcoming living/dining area is a comfortable space in winter to lounge and unwind in. During summer glass doors open out to the patio for barbecues. The larger triangular window shows off the depth of the straw bale walls and looks across to the spa, a converted milk-chilling vat! The bales are infilled around the supporting structure of stringy-bark bush poles. Terracotta floor tiles act as a heat sink for the lower winter sun.

hOme truths

The owners, keen proponents of permaculture, had initially browsed through magazines and accumulated snippets of information for inspiration. They reveal that one half of the partnership wanted a 'conventional home generous in its proportions and significantly more comfortable in temperature and size than our last one'; the other half favoured a more 'hippy/alternative' approach. Their somewhat opposing views were resolved in a 'marriage between the very rustic, organic feel and the straight-lined conventional'.

The best homes – those raised on the foundations of healthy principles – stimulate our curiosity and excite our imagination. These special places attract like-minded people to their construction and often become inspirational landmarks for ecological living. This exemplary straw bale home is one such place. Pleasing to the eye and nurturing to the soul, it was created in collaboration with an architect and builder, both 'tuned in' to a couple's desire to bring about an 'environmentally sustainable house'.

Appearances can be deceptive – this building hides its 'light' under a straight face, layers of smooth mud making invisible the undulations of straw bale walls. 'We were happy to consider the use of "alternative" building materials', say the owners. 'It didn't necessarily have to be straw bale, it had to be a material that was low in embodied energy and that could be used in a solar passive way. Straw bales happen to fit these criteria exceptionally well.'

above: Rendered in lime and with recycled white-mahogany cladding, the front of the house is orientated to enjoy a sunny aspect and benefit from passive solar strategies. The windows and doors open right back to connect the interior with the outdoors.

The needs of the family, including two active boys, were also considered – the site in a Sydney bush suburb allowing space for games, recreation and a kitchen garden.

The couple spent a year meeting architects before finding Andrea Wilson who, in their words, was 'a breath of fresh air'. Andrea believes that 'good design is based on life, health and conviviality rather than the latest trends' and readily empathised with the 'eco-brief' that included the concept of a 'fairly open plan, with the kitchen as the central focus and a sense of bringing the outside in'. Her imaginative design integrated external living areas with four separate straw bale buildings. The main house includes an attic storey for the two boys and three smaller pavilions for a detached bedroom wing, a carport/shed and a games room. The kitchen is the epicentre of the house and successfully follows Andrea's tenet of the importance of the relationship between the kitchen and the outdoor living area. As one of the owners says, 'Home to me means a kitchen'. Andrea envisioned the whole area to 'feel very grounded, like a relaxed family compound'. The bedroom pavilion includes the bathrooms. For Andrea, 'Bathrooms are for sensual enrichment, they need to be earthy and very connected with the great outdoors. I actually prefer them to be outside altogether, but I don't get too many clients who go for that idea!' She almost got her wish – the two bathrooms have floor-to-ceiling sliding doors that open onto a secluded outdoor space with a water feature.

above and above left: The games pavilion, rendered in clay with a lime finish, is equipped with transparent roller doors, recycled red-mahogany shutters and generous eaves, which minimise the effect of rain on the natural render.

The harmonious facades with their sheltering eaves accommodate a number of eco-initiatives that are not immediately apparent. For instance, the sun's energy is harnessed by solar panels on the roof and when it rains water is channelled into tanks via enclosed 'leaf free' guttering. These tanks meet the water needs of a family of four. The house was oriented and constructed for passive solar gain so no artificial heating or cooling is required. Up to 45 per cent of heat loss in a house can be through the roof, so Solomit boards of straw were used for insulation.

Throughout the house virtually all the timber is recycled and required arduous cleaning and assembling. 'The elaborate roof construction also uses recycled timber – an interesting challenge, even to a bunch of very experienced German carpenters!' says builder Frank Thomas, who the owners valued as much for his 'open-minded approach' as for his professionalism.

Comfort was important to the owners: 'In winter we sometimes get sub-zero temperatures with frosts, but in summertime it is diabolically hot! The thermometer is regularly at 44 degrees Celsius, sometimes for days on end'. The reliance on passive solar design and the use of straw

The home truth: 'The walls and render are dead straight – most people need to be shown that the house is made out of straw bales!' To reduce the harmful effects of electromagnetic fields, metal conduits conceal electricity cables.

bales for temperature control might have raised a few qualms but the owners have no regrets: 'You hear about the insulation effect of straw bales, and we believed that it was going to work but, having never experienced a truly solar-passive designed house, we were quite simply stunned at the results. It really is beautifully warm in winter and cool in summer. Last year there was an 18-degree difference between the outside temperature of 44 and the inside one of 26. In winter it is hard to believe that the house is not heated'.

While the house, full of quality workmanship and eco-features, stands as something of a showcase for applying sound design principles to the straw bale medium, it is also importantly a 'living' home, full of family life. As the owners say, 'We like our place to feel lived in, a place where both adults and children feel welcome. The house is great for having people over, especially during the warmer months when we just open up and our entertaining space is increased enormously'. Andrea, who must surely be gratified to hear that her design is home to 'life, health and conviviality', adds, 'I was really pleased with the owners' commitment to making a sustainable house but, ultimately, I know they love the place and that's the important result'.

above: Both bathrooms open out to a secluded outdoor space.

right: The owners love 'the way the bathrooms are very outdoor when the screens slide open, connecting them to the courtyard garden'.

facing page: A dash of pebble adds to that outdoors feel. To keep the straw bales moisture-free, the bathrooms were designed with the plumbing as a feature rather than built into the walls.

left: Playing with niches in a small room. When the translucent exterior door to the bathroom slides open it seals the porthole (a terracotta pipe insert).

below: A harmonious colour balance, with a soft purple wash and warm, earth tones. The wood surround is recycled tallowwood.

facing page: Softly curved recesses, deep window sills and feature niches are hallmarks of a straw bale construction: 'There are so many great spots within the house that when I stop for a quiet cuppa it is often hard to decide where exactly to sit and enjoy the quiet moment'

right: 'We like the simplicity of the design with the kitchen in the centre of the house. The boys love the space and the open plan.'

below: An open corner; the window seats, made from recycled Sydney blue gum, allow contemplation of the rear garden.

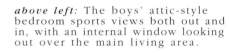

above left: The boys' attic-style bedroom sports views both out and in, with an internal window looking out over the main living area.

above: Solomit straw-boards form the roof insulation.

left: The narrow proportions of two salvaged doors dictated the unusual entrances to these two rooms; a log of reused white mahogany adds a step up. Ceilings and internal walls are Easiwall, a self-supporting, non-toxic insulating board made from wheat straw with a recycled paper liner – a slim product occupying far less floor space than straw bale.

facing page above: Permaculture and 'earthen' construction go hand in hand – fresh garden produce from the owners' permaculture garden.

facing page below: The kitchen emphasises the relationship with the outdoor living area, and is the focal space for cooking, eating and connecting with the outside. In winter the tiled floors absorb heat from the sun and release it slowly during the evening.

the romance of
s t o n e

'Stones are the bones
of heaven and earth.'

Ancient Chinese saying

If rock caves were our ancestors' first primitive shelters, how long did it take them to gather loose stone to form additional walls and dwellings? We can only speculate, but there is evidence to suggest that a circular gathering of stones discovered in northern Tanzania and dating back almost two million years was the foundation of an early building. At least no one can doubt the durability of a material millions of years old. There's the stone legacy left by the megalithic builders in their pagan sites, and processed stone-work, such as the Egyptian pyramids and Incan buildings, has also endured over thousands of years. The Egyptians overcame problems associated with the transportation of heavy stone, but pragmatic cultures draw on resources closer to home. Districts can be defined by their use of a local asset, buildings taking on a regional appearance with evocative connotations. For example, we associate granite with the rugged cottages and barns of Cornwall and the softer texture of sandstone with Sydney terrace houses. Some cultures have valued the material for reasons other than its use for building. An ancient Chinese gardening tradition appreciates stone for ornament and symbolism. Today stone is an expensive, unrenewable resource – we treasure and restore existing buildings but a whole house of newly quarried rock is not a sensible proposition. Consider smaller and alternative uses for stone in your living environments: 'rubblestone' makes attractive walls, and a traditional dry-stone wall or inviting stepping stones can become an eye-catching feature. Even one well-chosen rock can have a strong visual effect. Remember how Japanese gardens can say so much with so little?

previous page: These cliff-top houses in Sydney, Australia, were constructed with whatever was close to hand: loose stone, salvaged materials and driftwood. They have weathered with the seascape – sitting quietly in their wild environs.

above: Every piece of this dry-stone garden wall at Ratagan in the Scottish Highlands invites contemplation – the builder, with skill and intuition, balancing size and colour in harmonious pattern.

right: A collection of small stones form a delightfully rough-toothed hole, framing nature – an inspired portal for garden visitors to step through.

stone features

Every stony face tells a story, an ancient history of the land expressed through texture, colour, strata and grain. Have you ever seen a piece of stone without aesthetic appeal? Such appearances do not require make-up – theirs is a natural finish. Stone can be dressed perhaps with hammer and chisel but is undemanding of our paint and plaster.

Stone has advantages beyond its aesthetic appeal.

▼ It is a hardy construction material.

▼ Stone generally weathers well and age adds character.

▼ Stone holds heat, a useful asset in passive solar design.

▼ It combines well with other materials; marriages with timber and earth appear natural.

▼ Structures made from stone feel secure and imply permanence.

▼ Stone invites us to touch and encourages connection with the earth.

▼ It has durability and a visual appeal that can lend itself to a variety of applications.

When sourcing stone, remember that local stone will look better in your surrounds than imported material. Besides, long-distance transport adds to energy costs. Consider tracking down demolition and construction waste or fieldstone cleared from agricultural land to avoid damage to machinery. Salvage yards also offer dismantled and ruined building stone.

Be aware, however: some stones are better left unturned. Avoid disturbing river beds and protected natural areas. Check with the appropriate authorities before taking material from disused quarries and roadsides.

art house

a collaborative sculpture

Artists David Fairbairn and Suzanne Archer are renowned for their bold, energetic and fearless approach to painting, attributes that payed off handsomely when they applied them to the creation of their rugged home. The duo, who often create art pieces together, consider the building 'their most significant collaboration'.

Situated on the outskirts of Sydney in a pocket of natural bushland overlooking a rocky gorge, the cottage was built using stone found on the property and 'sits comfortably in the surroundings, becoming part of the landscape', as the owners intended. Through an honest use of materials and an expansive roof line over generous verandahs, the house suggests that a 'welcoming spirit' informed its design. Stepping over the threshold means 'security and comfort' to David and Suzanne after five years of building and temporary accommodation on-site. Their strong personalities infuse a cheering interior, rich in texture, ornament and decoration.

The home drew inspiration from a friend's stone house. Suzanne recalls, 'They had used the slip-form technique and we realised it was a process that aesthetically appealed to us and would reflect our bush setting. We also thought it was an affordable process that could be done in stages using plenty of stone from our property'. In discussion with their architects, an interesting, open-plan layout across two levels was devised. David elaborates: 'The house is made up of three connected stone buildings. The main living/kitchen space has an open cathedral ceiling higher than those of the two bedrooms, which are more intimate spaces. The living area and sleeping rectangles are connected by an enclosed walkway, which also serves as an office. The bathroom is attached to this. All the spaces were intended to have a function, a sense of life and an easy connection to the outdoors'.

The couple were mindful of resources in their drought-prone area and installed a dry composting Rota Loo to conserve water. They took an inventive approach with a diverse range of recycled materials including railway sleepers for exposed lintels, old timber posts from an old woolshed for roof support and a wonderful variety of salvaged doors and windows.

With summer temperatures reaching 30 degrees Celsius the extended roof line keeps the sun off the walls. In winter, when it can get down to 1 degree Celsius, the stone walls retain the heat from the slow-combustion stove.

Furnishings include an astonishing assortment of treasured objects and cultural artefacts collected on travels, with many of Suzanne and David's own distinctive works enjoying display. Asked to express how they feel now that the house is finished, Suzanne says there is 'a sense of incredible satisfaction and disbelief that we actually completed it'. David adds, 'It was such an enjoyable project to do together, like a huge collaborative sculpture'.

above: Unusually shaped windows and doors provide light and access to the main bedroom. A grand salvaged table doubles for informal outdoor dining and work, although most painting takes place in two studios, separate from the house.

above right: The house opens to beautiful outdoor living spaces – sheltered places to revive in sun-dappled surrounds. Pavers and gravel add a textured 'bridge' to the immediate bush and, unlike concrete, allow any rainwater to revive the land.

facing page: A bold approach to colour and surfaces in the stunning kitchen. Shallow, open shelving gives easy access to frequently used ingredients. For the owners, the space is 'generous and functional, easy to clean and great for entertaining'. The stainless steel is part custom-built, part reused.

above: Rooms extend naturally to the outdoor spaces. The surrounding bushland inspired the collaborative linocut print.

right: The main bedroom enjoys the sun's rays, often filtered through coloured glass insets. Window proportions are chosen to suit room size, walls 'bagged' in a softening ochre with feature niches. An obsolete dentist's cabinet is rejuvenated and adapted for clothes storage. Suzanne's vibrant collages sit with artefacts and fabrics from tribal cultures including those of Asia, Australia and Africa.

above: The main living space and dining area has a double-stone feature wall – ideal for ethnic artefacts, collaborative earthy-toned linocut prints and some lively collages.

facing page: An invigorating mix of patterned and colourful furnishings in the living area complement one of Suzanne's dynamic paintings. The terracotta floor has timeless appeal but, say the couple, 'laying and grouting the floor tiles throughout was one of the hardest parts, together with pointing up the stone-work'.

left: Constructing the bathroom. In slip-form building (such as this), stones are placed flat against the insides of rectangular wooden boxes, sections clamped together to form the thickness of the walls. Smaller rubble and a concrete mix are then poured into the remaining space to bond the stones. When one section is dry the form is 'slipped' off and moved upwards to make the next course.

right: A close-up of inner walls. Reinforcing mesh is tied to steel rods, which are used to strengthen the walls, particularly on corners. Conduits for power can also be built into the walls. Timber spacers and twisted bracing wire are used to hold the form sides equidistant at 300 millimetres. The wires also hold the forms off the ground as the wall is built up; they are cut off when the cement dries.

coastal
ROCK

and roll

The gritty entrance drive to Karkalla rises
and falls across a series of humps, shaped
with the aim of slowing vehicles approaching
the house and garden. While the undulations
look functional, they also have a more
subliminal reference to the forms of the dunes
and surf that fringe the Mornington Peninsula.

By the time visitors arrive and step from their cars the slow, roller-coastal ride has helped raise an awareness of the environmental sensibility that underpins the creation of this extraordinary coastal dwelling, home for Fiona Brockhoff and David Swann, and their young children. The property is located on the narrow tip of the Mornington Peninsula, residents and summer visitors enjoying the beaches of Port Phillip on one side and stretches of ocean-washed sands on the other. The windswept vegetated dunes of the region are in part protected by a national park that adjoins the property, and respect for the fragile ecology was a priority for Fiona, a landscape designer determined to 'tread softly on the land'. Her architect and builder, Thomas Isaksson, became a sympathetic collaborator who understood his client's desire to unify a house and garden, and to do so with minimal impact on the high sand dune.

'We have very similar tastes in architecture,' says Fiona, 'we both admire the work of Luis Barragan, and modernist Australian architecture of the 1950s and 1960s was a big influence. I had collected sketches and photos for a house over a long period

and Tom helped me interpret the ideas and bring them to life. We designed it in a weekend'. For Thomas the subsequent year spent on the building provided enduring memories: 'Fiona arranged a lot of labour from among her friends and there was a great camaraderie on the job'. He recalls, 'One day I looked out over Bass Strait from the roof and saw a fantastic swell coming in, then had the dawning realisation that the site was remarkably quiet – everyone had gone surfing!'

The prevailing weather conditions and the ocean's proximity, besides determining 'time out', had a profound effect on the aspect of the house and the choice of durable materials and finishes in the face of salty winds. Although the climate is deemed cool-temperate, Thomas says, 'The coast is often lashed by wild weather, so the building closes to the harsher elements and opens to the benign ones'.

The precise geometry of the structure provides a formal backdrop for the rough and tumble of the garden surrounds and, while the aesthetic appearance pays homage to the key features of mid-century modernism – with an added dash of Fiona's memories of a childhood spent in her family's 1950s home – the important underlying tenets are purely environmental.

above: The slope of the land is stepped with reclaimed pier supports. The living area and first-floor bedroom rise behind the entry wall, with magnificent bay views from the upper storey.

left: On the northern terrace some of the plantings close to the house include drought-tolerant shrubs and succulents. Fiona explains: 'I chose predominantly flora that was indigenous to the area. The use of other exotic species was an experiment; they didn't all work but I was not prepared to pamper anything'.

facing page: The limestone columns stand sentinel to the natural bush areas and were commissioned from New Zealand sculptor Chris Booth. Fiona: 'I like the fact that the garden picks up the hues and colours of the distant landscape, it's an extension of the surroundings with added pieces of interest'.

The house and garden were adjusted to the contours of the land, which minimised excavation and disturbance to the site, the changes of level and variously angled skillion roofs complementing the inclines of the surrounding dunes. The more open-faced living areas to the north benefit from the sun's penetration in winter; the rear of the house has slim windows to reduce exposure to the cold south-westerlies. There is a solar-powered hot-water system for the whole house and all rainfall is harvested from the roofs, providing for the house needs except in long periods of drought. Grey water is recycled, passing through an absorption trench system; the purified water rises through gravel by capillary action to nurture the organic garden. Dry composting toilets help build up the soil in other parts of the garden, and chickens, shared with a neighbour, process garden and household refuse to produce eggs and free fertiliser, a recommended permaculture practice.

'We tried to use as many recycled and locally sourced materials as possible', says Fiona, who had collected a large amount of New Zealand kauri pine and other secondhand timbers in anticipation of building. An existing fibro shack on-site was dismantled, many of its parts reused, and massive pier beams were salvaged – the sea-weathered timbers help define spaces in the extensive garden. The key component, though, is the white Sorrento limestone, a famous local resource used since early colonial times for building. The distinctive rock walls that connect the inside to the out were constructed by David, a landscape contractor.

The couple's achievement has been to sensitively integrate a most singular house and garden with the exposed surrounds, the process including conservation and restoration of the vulnerable bushland (the property is also a registered wildlife reserve). By working with the challenging conditions and enhancing the intrinsic qualities of the region, Fiona and David have succeeded in establishing a truly remarkable place that celebrates the indigenous ecology and coastal nature of the site.

The use of local limestone 'anchors' the house and garden to the landscape, and David's signature walls add protection to outdoor spaces. The rock is a facing on an inner core of hollow concrete blocks.

According to Fiona, 'The hub of the house is the living/kitchen area, which faces north for passive solar gain. Although we have gas-powered hydronic heating, I find that the house is warm anyway. There is natural wool insulation in the ceiling and floors'. Says Thomas, 'I think we realised our aim to create a strong architecture through simple, spatial manipulation and a balancing of different textural qualities'. The hearth, with its custom-made canopy, sits on a cantilevered concrete bench that extends, along with the limestone wall, out to the northern terrace. Windows throughout the house are either double-glazed or thickened to retain heat, and aluminium framing was chosen for durability against the salt-laden air.

facing page: The recently completed guest bungalow borrows design themes from the main house. 'Now that the planting has matured, it is becoming more difficult to say whether the landscape forms a backdrop for the architecture, or vice versa. Either reading would be a success as far as I'm concerned', states Thomas.

left: A strip of intense blue in the kitchen suggests distant horizons, and the painter Mondrian might have approved of the concise arrangement of 'modern' geometrical forms.

below: An interplay of diverse textures in the guest bungalow includes a feature wall of rough 'free masonry', a ceiling lined with natural pine strips, and gloss-finished kitchen surfaces.

touching on Wood

Nature supplies us with another renewable building material – timber, appropriated for a variety of structures since primitive times. Branches and leaves were used by our hunter-gatherer ancestors in temporary shelters, a continuing tradition among remaining tribes of nomadic bush people. Although constructions using wood are prone to fire, pests and moisture, there are many timber buildings that have endured the test of time, including a Japanese Buddhist temple built in the seventh century and English cottages from the fourteenth century. Timber has always been valued as an easy-to-use, versatile resource, one that embodies the term 'natural material – a true organic matter.

Oyster sticks and reclaimed piers are full of character but require a flexible construction approach. Architect Clinton Murray explains: 'Each of the posts and beams had to be hand-chosen for their position; some, being slightly twisted, were out of alignment from top to bottom by up to several inches'. Patience was rewarded: the acclaimed result is shown on page 155.

We hardly need encouragement to 'go with the grain' but, used wisely, timber:

▼ has numerous structural and aesthetic applications from support posts, framing and furniture to panelling and trims

▼ adds character and natural warmth, with old timbers and salvaged woods telling many a story

▼ can be reused, recycled and finished in many ways

▼ absorbs sound and regulates indoor air humidity

▼ has a wonderful, sensory appeal with its variety of colours, grains, textures and scents.

Once in plentiful supply, timber is now a rapidly diminishing resource with half of the world's forests decimated and the remaining ones virtually unprotected. Old-growth woodlands and ancient rainforest tracts cannot be replaced; they are important for their biodiversity and wildlife, and also provide special recreational spaces. We should be extremely concerned about the continuing loss of these ecological environs and support international organisations working to prevent their disappearance. While in theory timber is renewable, in practice demand outstrips supply, the problems associated with unsustainable usage compounded by illegal land-clearing. Reforestation projects and better-managed plantation growth aim to redress the ecological imbalance, but there is a need to look at how we use the resource, particularly in building as '55 per cent of the wood cut for non-fuel uses is for construction',[11] and 'a standard wood-framed house consumes over one acre of forest and the waste created during construction averages from 3 to 4 tonnes'.[12] Clearly ways of building that reduce reliance on timber are an imperative.

good wood practices

Start with the choice of reused, recycled or non-timber materials for construction – several are outlined in this book. The reclaiming of used timber has minimal environmental impact and there are many reasons to leave trees standing, including their ability to improve atmospheric quality through the reduction of carbon dioxide.

We can also consider the use of timber from sustainably managed plantations. These products should carry an appropriate stamp certifying that they originate from a renewable resource.

Other sound timber tactics include:

▼ looking for ways to reduce the amount of timber used in a house

▼ using unprocessed timber where 'minimal processing' and no wastage are suitable, such as log houses and where round wood is used for support

▼ using radial sawing to maximise the use of a log, which, compared with conventional cutting, uses up to 20 per cent more of each log (the process also applies to small logs)

▼ buying secondhand timber furniture instead of selecting new items made from wood of dubious origin

▼ briefing your builder and architect to specify for sustainability and forest-friendly timbers

▼ using local instead of imported timbers to better suit the regional climate and landscape

▼ keeping the embodied energy of timber low by avoiding long-distance transportation.

When constructing, remember that wood is susceptible to moisture and prone to attack from pests and insects. Ensure that your building is properly constructed to minimise these threats. Seek out eco-alternatives for the treatment of wood, as many conventional products are highly toxic. Timber finishes and preservatives often contain compounds such as arsenic and copper chromium, which are bad for your health and the environment. Urea formaldehyde or phenol is sometimes used for the bonding of composite timber boards. Noxious fumes released from these boards (known as off-gassing) can present a serious health problem, as can dust released from the cutting of such treated timber.

Informed purchasing can have an important effect on the timber industry and thoughtful choices will support manufacturers and producers who have changed to better practices. As consumers we can ask ourselves and our suppliers the right questions to ensure that what we intend to buy has the right credentials – have your say in the future of the world's forests.

Salvaged bridge supports come with their own history and personality. While working with salvaged timber can be harder – old nails need to be removed and the inconsistency of sizes requires ingenuity – the process reminds us to construct with an eye to the future, using methods that can be easily deconstructed at a later date.

The ecologically sound Treetops in the Tweed Valley has
its own reforestation program on the property where
Griffith Furniture mill salvaged logs into flitches before
they are stabilised in a solar kiln. Whole slabs of wood are
often used for furniture with little wastage. Traditional
techniques of construction avoid nails and glue, creating
fully demountable furniture, which simplifies transport and
the replacement of components.

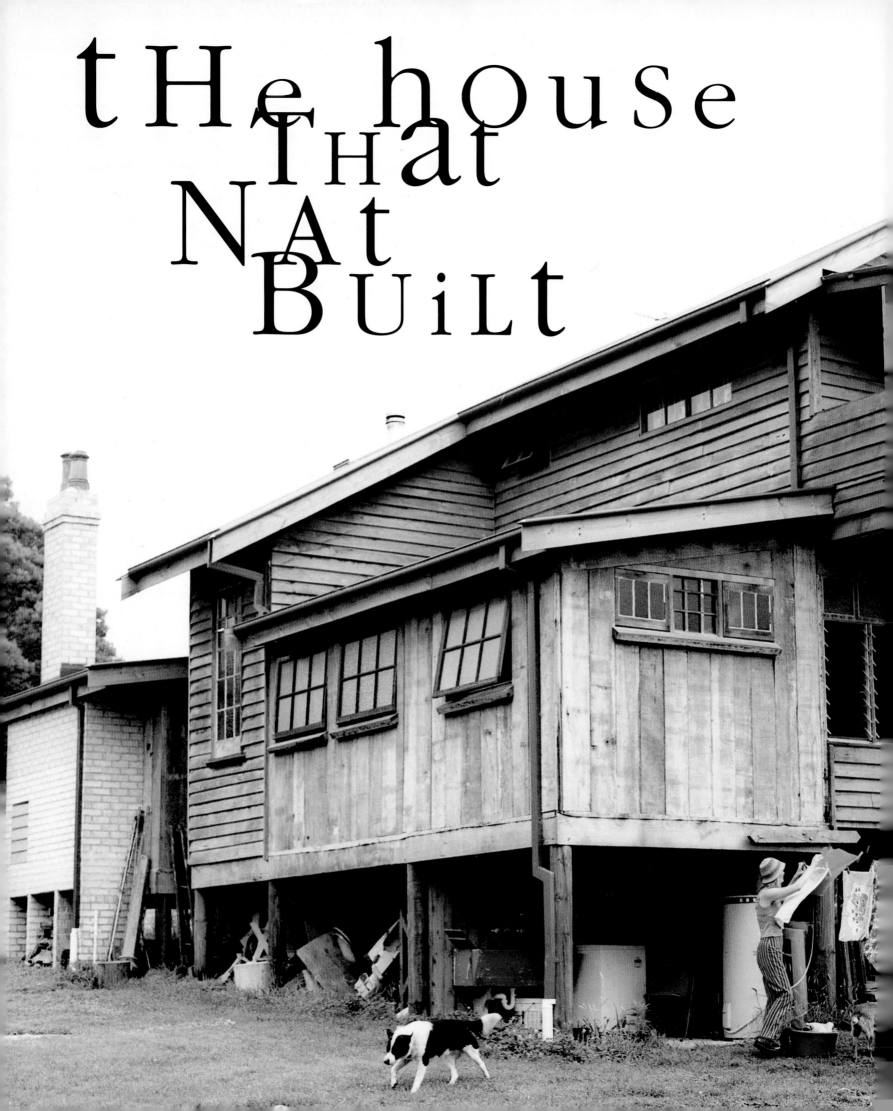

tHe hoUSe THat NAt BUiLt

The rugged, down-to-earth character of furniture maker Nat Curnow is writ large across his own dwelling, an idiosyncratic structure that tells us the owner is passionate about timber and the straightforward, honest use of the stuff.

The cantilevered verandahs and simple slab-wall construction reveal an appreciation of old colonial Australian buildings and their joinery methods. The striking appearance of the place also reflects the owner's penchant for Robert Mitchum movies, as Nat clarifies: 'The ones set in the mid-west, where the high-sided houses have steep pitch roofs'. Suggestions from some neighbours that there's a hint of the setting for Hitchcock's *Psycho* have been received with good humour.

The maverick Nat once had a renowned furniture shop in Sydney and chanced upon this property, with its ruinous 1920s ice-making shed, on a weekend excursion down the South Coast of eastern Australia. He had been considering a 'sea change' from city living and the rustic, utilitarian construction with its dirt floor beckoned as a rough and ready workshop. The fact that the three-phase power necessary for his woodworking machinery could be easily installed helped clinch the deal.

Defining the entrance boundary of the property with a dry-stone wall was the first step for Nat and his partner, Seána Ryan. The couple recall, 'There was a sign, "free bush rock", on a nearby farmer's land so we took the ute and brought back loads of it, building about a metre of wall each weekend'.

Seána Ryan 'hangs out' with the two dogs. All the water collected from the high pitched roofs and the original ice-making shed is stored in tanks that can hold up to 20,000 gallons. The fish-shaped balusters on the decks refer to Nat's passion for fishing; the vertical hardwood slabs on the lower level of the house pay tribute to simple 'pioneer' construction methods and are walls for the bathroom and guest bedroom.

left: The dry-stone boundary wall has a timeless feel: 'Because it is weathered local rock and naturally constructed, people think it is an original part of the property'. The old ice-making shed in the foreground, with the trusty ute parked outside, has been extended in keeping with its original rustic look.

right: The picturesque spare bedroom with the 'pioneer' slab walls. The coloured ceiling boards came from a demolition in Sydney and are left in their found state. 'I took them out of the house myself', says Nat, 'I wanted the old paint finish'. The old meat safe 'came from a country house verandah – the kind where people turn their homes into antique shops', says Nat, who also snapped up the 1950s clock and model of a traditional sailing boat.

Resourceful and practical doesn't begin to describe the self-taught furniture maker who had accumulated three semi-trailer loads of salvaged timbers – raw materials for his custom-made pieces. This stock went into the making of the three-bedroom house. Commonsense underlies its design and orientation, the structure poised above the slope at the front and connected with the land at the rear by an entrance deck and patio. The raised elevation of both floors allows views over the surrounding countryside, and the living areas benefit from the sun's path.

The quirky verandahs 'help protect the house and are little areas to sit in the sun, out of the wind'. The varied windows, doors, fixtures and furnishings are a result of this inveterate collector's forays around markets, country sales and auction houses. The home bears the hallmarks of Nat's one-off furniture pieces, displaying his uncanny knack of integrating and proportioning diverse elements into a pleasing unity.

After completing his first house, the establishment of a flourishing fruit and vegetable garden was but a minor challenge to the former New Zealand landscaper, who has cultivated nashi pears, peaches, lemons, oranges, feijoas, passionfruit vines, macadamia nuts and a kaffir lime tree in the surrounds. He and Seána now have young Reuben and Patrick to nourish. 'The garden supplies pretty close to all our needs,' states Nat, 'although I got a shock in the last drought when I had to actually buy some vegetables.'

The home was not intended as an environmentally focused construction, but a keen observation of the land and respect for materials have brought about the same. The eccentric appearance of the place may not conform to 'standard' living – homes are, after all, an intensely personal form of expression – yet you cannot help but admire the knowledge, imagination and endeavour that have gone into its shaping.

above: Unconventional room proportions are a good foil for the bold use of colours inspired by cartoon books. 'I thought, why not? It's only paint and we can always go over it again if it doesn't work', says Nat. Exposed beams of Oregon accentuate the roof pitch and a salvaged piece of wrought iron with a chunky architrave makes an unusual frame for the floor-level aperture on the upper landing. The assorted furniture and paintings are singularly disparate but held together by the same fearless aesthetic.

right: In front of the slow-combustion stove the 'striped' floor of the living room carries a 1940s patterned wool rug. The sliding doors lead to the study, a snug retreat that has a pressed-tin ceiling and a fireplace for the coldest days.

above top: This sturdy cabinet has a cheerful setting: left unrestored, it shows its history in the marks, scratches and repairs accumulated over the years.

above: Nat's eclectic treasures decorate the house: 'When I first arrived in Australia, antiques and bric-a-brac were plentiful. I used to do the markets, just collecting things for the shop – rising sun jugs, all kinds of amazing crockery'.

right: The Federation door to Seána's studio and the spare bedroom has dimpled glass panes in green and gold. Louvred windows provide cross-ventilation.

Inside the bathroom, wall timbers are oiled to bring out the grain, and joints sealed with silicone to allow for movement in the humidity. Nat found the slabs through an advert: 'For me, one of the beauties of a slab wall is that you stand it up and it's done. There's less framing, finishing and insulation. It's a good look, and quick, uncomplicated and easy'.

The generous stairwell leads to the two upper bedrooms. Behind the adjacent hefty slab walls is the bathroom; its Victorian panelled door has been glazed with glass from a 1950s shower-screen. Nat's intuitive mix of styles often leads to interesting dynamics: the interlocking 1950s pattern is echoed in the form of the staircase.

above: Border collie 'LB' and the kauri pine floorboards share an interesting 'patched' appearance. Nat believes in the minimal processing and cutting of materials with an eye to their future reuse: 'I like the original finish. Most people sand their boards back and put polyurethane on, which isn't very recyclable – the boards often glue together. It's not a nice way to go'.

facing page: The old Baltic pine cabinet in the living room was rescued from a liquidation sale in the Snowy Mountains, the distressed paint finish seeming to reference its previous location.

sustaining family life

These extraordinary houses are part of a remarkable family compound for the Murrays, three generations living on one parcel of land. The original home, for Max and Gwen Murray, can be glimpsed off to the right, with a first-floor office added for architect Clinton, one of their four sons. The curiously shaped 'Caravan of Dreams', with its exclamation-mark window, is next – built by and for another of their sons, Andrew, and his wife, Margot, and their two daughters, Alex and Kate. Across the yard, with its unique tower, is the 'House for Pam'. This is home for Clinton and Pam, and their four sons, Max, Miles, Oliver and Solomon. These three additions and a number of neighbouring houses in the picturesque Australian coastal town of Merimbula were designed by Clinton, built by Andrew and overseen by their father, Max.

The rear yard and garden of the family enclave. The eagle atop the tower – poised above the garden – functions as a water spout. 'Over 20 years we've grown a fair bit in the garden', says Andrew. 'It started off as just sand so I built up the soil with anything you can imagine: seaweed; ostrich, chicken, sheep, cow and horse manure; ribbony weed; worms; fish meal; hay and grass clippings; and just stuff – the soil is unbelievable now.'

There's always some new addition to admire when visiting the Murrays (if not to the buildings then to the family!). And why not? 'When a man is finished with his house, he's finished with life', says an old Chinese adage. In truth our homes are continually evolving, changing and developing – architecture is not as static as we imagine. Stewart Brand states 'all buildings grow', elaborating with 'domestic buildings ... are the steadiest changers, responding directly to the family's ideas and annoyances, growth and prospects. Homes are the domain of slowly shifting fantasies and rapidly shifting needs'.[13]

If this small enclave illustrates a wider truism, then the Murrays, with their collaborative skills in design and building, are well placed to adapt to changes, and to do so with style.

Close-knit family living is a tradition that Clinton enjoys. His great grandfather started a building company many years ago and his father, Max, continued the business. Clinton recalls fondly: 'Our families were living side by side in those days. All our homes were built by my grandfather and great uncle. The brothers all built their properties side by side. My grandfather and great aunt lived with us and we shared the garden and

driveway with my great uncle and aunt. All the houses backed onto the building yard, which took up the whole block'. In the 1980s Max and Gwen moved to the current property in 'semi-retirement'; Clinton and Andrew followed later. In recent years old customs were reinstated as Clinton's architectural practice took off, Max Murray Snr helping with the daily business and Andrew Murray an integral part of the construction process, adding creative touches to his brother's designs. As Pam notes, 'There were lots of clients getting great homes so I said to Clinton, "I wouldn't mind just a little tiny house!" He took a bit of persuading but finally designed one'.

The House of Pam, the newcomer to the block, is deceptively simple in design, 'boxing clever' in minimal appearance. Always intended as a comfortable family home, it was not conceived as an 'eco' structure as such. Nevertheless, the underlying commonsense in its making appealed to a jury from the Royal Australian Institute of Architects who gave it two awards, including one for ecologically sustainable design, citing that the building, with its use of reclaimed timbers and natural ventilation, 'delivers so much towards sustainability'.

Natural elements and angles in a quiet corner deck behind the tower. Andrew often adds textures into areas of paving: 'The cement floors and this wall were done with a dimpled roller, invented for the purpose. I've played with many things to get textures – pressing in frozen fish, casuarina leaves, rolling banksia cones. I've used power plugs, goanna feet, lambs' feet, just about anything that gives an interesting effect'.

The living room and boys' room. Pam says, 'Clinton designed enough space in the boys' room for them to have their stuff in there; they make a big mess and it doesn't really affect us in the living room'.

'The kids' room is more than just a bedroom. They spend a lot of time in there, yet feel quite connected to us with the kitchen adjacent. There is more floor space because the beds are off the floor and the boys can get to their room from the deck', says Pam.

'We weren't sure about a black wall', say Pam and Clinton. 'We went away for a day and said to Bill and Andrew, "Please don't paint it black", but when we returned it was black. We really liked it! Because it's a large space it seems to take the colour.'

left: Spaces are defined by light, here filtered through the surrounding trees, which inspired the green wall colour. Eight different colours were used to get the mottled effect.

The house makes admirable use of available 'family' land, and the children benefit from the proximity of relatives. The home centres around the living/kitchen area, which is flanked by the boys' room and a secluded deck at one end, the main bedroom at the other. The intriguing tower, something of an architectural Trojan horse, was designed as a 'retreat' and captures glorious coastal views. For Clinton, 'The House for Pam was tricky given that it's so close to my parents' and brother's houses. It is designed so as to not overcrowd the existing homes and to not clash visually – forms were kept simple'.

The flooring and the exterior cladding (as well as some of the interior cladding) are reclaimed Oregon and the window frames are recycled hardwood timbers. Clinton explains, 'The Oregon boards were reclaimed from a 1940s factory in Sydney. It was used there as a ceiling liner, 42 millimetres thick, tongue and grooved'. The huge sliding windows look out over the front garden and saw-tooth windows in the roof capture winter sun. During colder months underfloor heating in the concrete kitchen and bathroom areas warms the house. On hot and still summer days ventilation is buoyancy-driven by the tower.

facing page (left inset): The house was originally conceived for a family of four but even new arrival Oliver gets a stylish sleeping quarter.

facing page (right inset): Outside the kitchen door, the water tank was custom-built to suit the available space.

above: 'I like the siting of the kitchen. It gets the sun directly in the morning and is also a central point, a focus of the house. The storage is really neat, the big drawers just open out and you can see all of the crockery', says Pam. The louvred windows provide cross-ventilation and views of the children when they play in the yard.

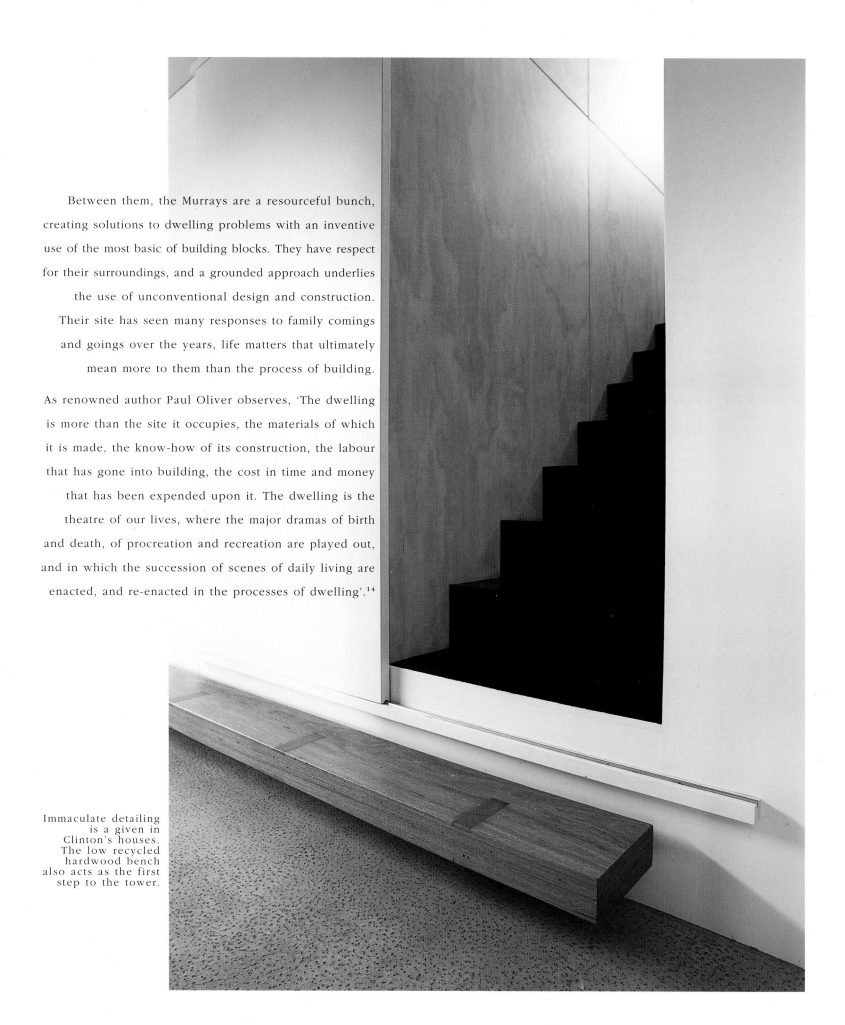

Between them, the Murrays are a resourceful bunch, creating solutions to dwelling problems with an inventive use of the most basic of building blocks. They have respect for their surroundings, and a grounded approach underlies the use of unconventional design and construction. Their site has seen many responses to family comings and goings over the years, life matters that ultimately mean more to them than the process of building.

As renowned author Paul Oliver observes, 'The dwelling is more than the site it occupies, the materials of which it is made, the know-how of its construction, the labour that has gone into building, the cost in time and money that has been expended upon it. The dwelling is the theatre of our lives, where the major dramas of birth and death, of procreation and recreation are played out, and in which the succession of scenes of daily living are enacted, and re-enacted in the processes of dwelling'.[14]

Immaculate detailing is a given in Clinton's houses. The low recycled hardwood bench also acts as the first step to the tower.

'During design the tower changed quite a lot', explains Clinton. 'It took me a while to work out what to do with the windows – I designed things so that we didn't overlook the other buildings. The windows are positioned so that you look out, not down. The one on this lower level is placed to get the nor-easterly and works beautifully; it cools the whole tower down.' A hatch in the roof allows air through, part of the stack-cooling design.

above: Sensational 360-degree coastal views from the tower: here, the view shows the main beach of Merimbula and the house across the road, designed by Clinton, making use of recycled wharf timbers.

left: 'We never did get our retreat – the boys have taken over the tower!' laughs Pam. Clinton adds, 'The colours were inspired by Cuisenaire rods; we were taught to count with them when we were children in the 1960s and I collect them'.

facing page: Hidden, narrow steps give access to the top floor in the tower and the final deck ladder. The tower's colour and construction give a feeling of being in a Rubik's cube. 'The first floor became a holding bay for the new babies, first Oliver and now Solomon. Max has appropriated the top', says Clinton.

Family life continues in the Caravan of Dreams, where Margot, Andrew, Kate and Alex look across to the tower and talk about their part of the enclave. Andrew tells the story: 'In the 1920s the house that was here was an old butcher's shop. In the 1950s someone cut it up and put an extension on the front so it was two separate houses. When I came to live here it had pink floral wallpaper and was repulsive, so we slapped some paint on it to make it semi-liveable and started to play with the house a bit. We were pushed for space and I remember saying to Clinton, "We'd like to have a new kitchen and dining room, perhaps you could incorporate this stainless steel sink that I've collected?" That was the brief. He came up with a drawing and we looked at it and I thought, my god! I just expected a regular extension but the shape looked totally stupid – it was a drawing of a caravan! So I thought, well, Clinton knows what he is doing and I love caravans, trains and planes, so it was up to me to build it. First of all we had the shape. We had no idea what we were going to clad it with. There was some left-over plywood from another house that we had used as a floor so we thought, okay, we might as well use that on the wall. It's all plywood inside, there's no plaster – things just evolved. I really like Zincalume steel as a material and thought that would be a good idea; no one else has clad a house in zinc like that'. (He might have added that no one else has ever had a house like that!)

above left: 'I designed their extension to recall childhood holidays at the Eden caravan park, with a twist. Light, ventilation and theatre were all important elements as it is here that many of our design discussions are carried out', says Clinton. Margot adds, 'It's always exciting watching people's reactions'. A ramp leads to the quirky door with its six portholes, and steps have since been fitted to the entrance on the left.

middle left: 'When you say to someone that your kitchen/dining room is 3 metres wide, 4 metres high and 18 metres long, they can't comprehend the shape,' says Andrew, 'but being in here – it's just bloody great. I feel completely at peace when I come in'.

below left: The vertical-wood trimmed doors cleverly interlock with the fascia, concealing storage space.

facing page: On one side of the kitchen a long row of blue asymmetrical cupboard doors are reference to Andrew's ears.

'At breakfast the morning sun hits the orange wall and it looks like it's on fire. You start the day with a splash of colour – you can't beat it. The table is made out of a scrap of ply and the legs are the base of a Charles Eames piece from the 1950s – probably the most expensive thing that I've bought', says Andrew.

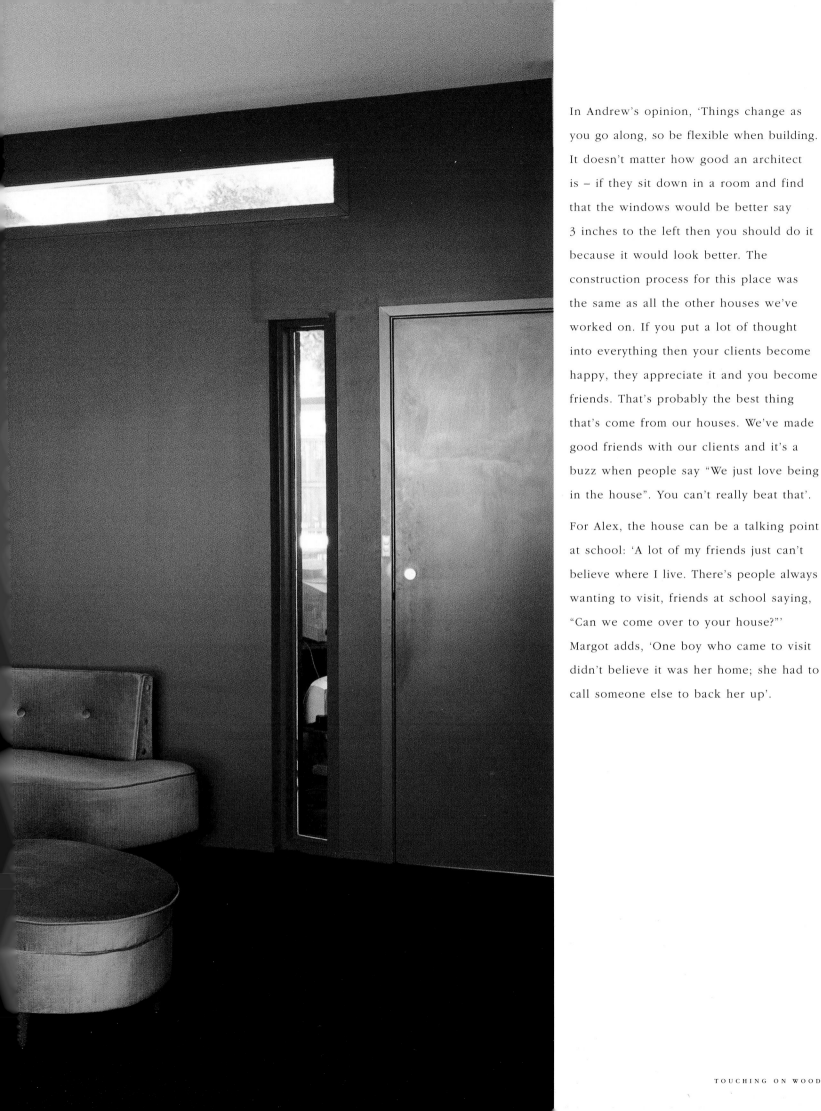

In Andrew's opinion, 'Things change as you go along, so be flexible when building. It doesn't matter how good an architect is – if they sit down in a room and find that the windows would be better say 3 inches to the left then you should do it because it would look better. The construction process for this place was the same as all the other houses we've worked on. If you put a lot of thought into everything then your clients become happy, they appreciate it and you become friends. That's probably the best thing that's come from our houses. We've made good friends with our clients and it's a buzz when people say "We just love being in the house". You can't really beat that'.

For Alex, the house can be a talking point at school: 'A lot of my friends just can't believe where I live. There's people always wanting to visit, friends at school saying, "Can we come over to your house?"' Margot adds, 'One boy who came to visit didn't believe it was her home; she had to call someone else to back her up'.

6 contemporary materials

how to use them wisely

An environmental, energy-efficient house can come in many guises, often using 'off the shelf', readily available materials and appliances to enhance its function. Mass-produced items, low in both cost and embodied energy, can be incorporated into contemporary dwellings that are designed to work with local climates and capable of providing for sustainable living. And while many would still favour a soundly built earthen structure to epitomise the ideal of a 'green' building, mud and straw construction methods are not always appropriate to a new site or applicable to the improvement and furnishing of an existing building.

For example, many dwellings are constructed with fired bricks that have high embodied energy, and it would be difficult to retro-fit them with earthen materials. By careful selection of contemporary materials, however, it is possible to convert these structures into models of sustainability. Michael Mobbs and his family have, for instance, transformed a very traditional-looking brick terraced house in Sydney into a virtually self-sufficient home, one that harvests rainwater, generates its own power and recycles black and grey water on-site. The renovation involved thorough consideration of the safety of additional materials, and 'efficiency' was key to their choice of appliances.

It is important to evaluate the primary environmental costs of contemporary materials and appliances in the broader context of a building's life-cycle and ongoing energy costs, and seek ways to reduce their impact. If, for example, we choose concrete flooring, a material relatively high in embodied energy, will the use of its thermal mass to reduce reliance on artificial heating during the house's life span offset the initial ecological cost? Are there ways to minimise the use and impact of a given resource?

Substituting flyash, slag or even rice husks – all waste materials – for cement can lower the embodied energy of concrete. Instead of solid concrete walls we could consider aerated or lightweight concrete blocks, which use far less material in their making. Popular in Europe since the 1960s, they have good compressive strength and offer better insulation than concrete, which make them an ideal choice for some wall applications. Looking for alternatives can benefit the environment, improve energy efficiency and reduce our long-term expenditure.

off the shelf

Always begin with a design and specifications appropriate to the site and climate. The choice of materials and appliances follow from this tenet. Choose materials that are biodegradable, non-toxic, low in embodied energy, and from renewable resources. Durability is important, as short-life products result in greater environmental impact. Seek and assess information given by suppliers on their specification and safety sheets. As a rule of thumb when reading product descriptions, words worth consideration begin with 're', as in 'this product reuses, recovers, rescues, reconstitutes, recycles or reclaims waste materials in its construction'. Be wary of 'greenwash', information that presents a product as being environmentally sound when it may not be – for example, a reconstituted flooring material that uses recycled waste might sound good, but is not if, in manufacture, it was bonded with a noxious compound. Avoid products where the information supplied does not satisfy – manufacturers do respond to consumer purchasing patterns.

Consider off-the-shelf secondary materials and furnishings that contain raw constituents and agricultural by-products. These can be manufactured from sustainable crops using low-impact technology and non-toxic additives. For example, bamboo is a popular biodegradable alternative for flooring. Glueless laminate floorings low in embodied energy are available; they contain post-consumer recycled content, industrial waste and materials from sustainable resources. Hemp boards and coir matting from coconut husks are both made using agricultural by-products – coir matting can be backed with natural rubber. Investigate straw boards for walling and insulation; they are often treated with natural salts for fire resistance. Shop for insulation that recycles waste products, rags and paper, and also those products that contain wool and cellulose fibres. In textiles look for materials using natural fibres with environmentally considerate production methods. Be aware that some processes use formaldehyde, harmful bleaches and various chemicals. When choosing cotton products look for 'organic' labels, as pesticides and chemicals are often part of conventional cotton-growing methods. Finish your surfaces with healthy alternatives: for final exterior and internal coatings choose paints, sealers and finishes that are organic, natural and non-toxic.

sheds light

form + function = a new unity

When ceramicist Brigitte Enders and glass artist Klaus Moje considered building a place to house their family of two boys and provide workrooms for themselves, they knew that space was a prerequisite. As Brigitte states, 'We just needed it big, and 24 by 12 metres sounded just right!' The measurements refer to the floor size of their shed, an opportune find at an industrial auction, setting the couple back only A$2500. Klaus gives a wry smile when he recalls that 'the price was a fraction of the amount that we had to pay to have three-phase power installed', a critical requirement for their studio kilns. The purchase, besides meeting their spatial requirements and offering an affordable choice, was also an expression of their aesthetic preferences. 'Other options were too "cosy" for our taste', says Brigitte. 'We liked the idea of a utilitarian structure, a given format to play with.'

The home, located on the invigorating Sapphire Coast of New South Wales, is reached through a copse of eucalypts, the dirt track twisting down and emerging from the trees into a sequestered pastoral valley – a small lake and five head of cattle complete the idyll. There are stacks of salvaged building materials stored by the drive, a common feature of many resourceful country dwellings. The customised shed backs up to the wood and is angled to view the lush countryside, its outward appearance resembling one of the farm outbuildings that stud the region.

The reuse of an easily dismantled steel structure was a smart idea, minimising waste and the consumption of any new building materials. The doors and windows were salvaged from junkyards: 'We built the shed and then worked out where they might go', says Brigitte. The siting of the large picture windows to aid the accumulation of passive solar energy could not have been better, although Brigitte admits that the orientation of the house was 'instinctive', and the beneficial heat retention of the concrete floor attributable to luck: 'We actually liked the look of a polished concrete floor'.

Whether by luck or intuition, the floor functions remarkably well as a heat-sink in the cool-temperate climate. 'In winter', says Brigitte, 'the sun goes two-thirds of the way into the house'. The stored warmth is slowly released in the evening and held within the building by two layers of reflective ceiling insulation, left visible in keeping with the functional look. The insulation also stops the shed overheating in summer, and the extended roof line shields the floor from the sun in the warmer seasons. All the water they need is harvested from the roof and stored in two tanks.

Brigitte's workroom sheds
light on a peaceful, bucolic
setting. The placement of
the doors are practical and
visually satisfying – form
following function. The
arched 'keyhole' door was
salvaged from a house-
breaker's yard and brings
a rounded edge to the
uniformity of the corrugated
'production lines'.

The classic vintage Citröens are emblematic of the design aesthetics and functionality that this home is founded on. The windows offer uninterrupted views across the lush countryside and lake. 'We made a deliberate decision not to put any planting out front,' says Brigitte, 'no pots, barbecues or chairs'.

When it came to subdividing the structure, the couple say, 'We deliberately chose opposite ends for each of our studios', (a move prompted by an earlier experience when they shared a confined work space!). Hollow concrete bricks are used to wall the two workrooms, each measuring 12 by 6 metres and equipped with internal and external access doors. The remainder of the floor space is given over to an open-plan living/dining/kitchen area, with a smaller portion set aside at the rear for the main bedroom, access corridor and bathroom. The generous ceiling height suggested the idea of a mezzanine, big enough for the boys' bedrooms, illuminated by skylights and with internal windows over the central living area.

The division of space is well considered and disarmingly simple, the choice and location of the windows and doors admirably suiting the proportions of the structure. The interior is clean-cut and spare, walls devoid of superfluous mouldings and embellishments, epitomising the description 'contemporary and modern'. An uncomplicated look perhaps, but engineering it proved more demanding than the couple imagined as many builders found the idea of adapting an industrial structure for living a difficult concept to grasp. As Brigitte recalls, 'Some builders seemed to have a "shed" mentality – getting the right standard and quality of workmanship was very hard'. This must have been a frustration for the couple whose own personal work springs from a combination of inspiration and well-founded technical knowledge, with attention to detail and finish an essential part of the process.

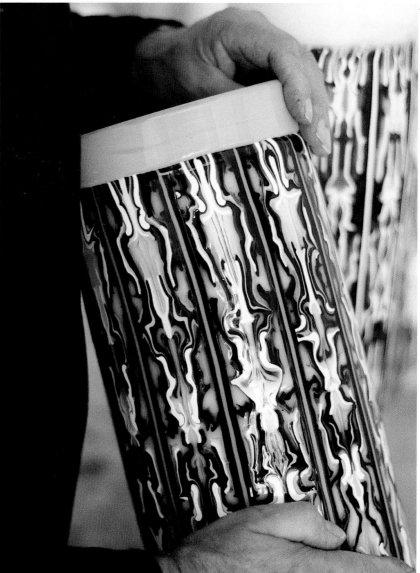

above: Klaus first exhibited mosaic vessels in 1975 and his contemporary interpretation of this ancient Hellenistic technique has gained him world-wide renown. In Australia his palette has intensified, affected by the vibrant colour and light of his new surroundings.

left: The intricate mosaic pattern on Klaus's distinctive work is created by pre-fusing a number of strips into one large panel, which is then rolled into cylindrical form with a contrasting band of colour at each end.

facing page: Let there be light – and colour: the raw materials for Klaus's glasswork seen through the door to his studio. The walls, featuring a bold woodcut by Hap Grieshaber, were left unplastered, the form of the concrete blocks visible.

right and below: There are softening touches in Brigitte's studio including a harpsichord and a recliner – cat napping is allowed in this workspace. Brigitte studied ceramics and industrial design and her work, seen here on the cupboards, exhibits an integration of various disciplines and techniques. Many of her pieces, defined by exquisite refinement and distillation of form, are held in international museums and galleries.

The design axioms applied to the home reveal the couple's training and background, and reference the guiding principles of the Bauhaus, an institution founded in Germany by architect Walter Gropius in 1918. His school reacted to social change after World War I to develop a new rationale for architecture, 'pure forms' arising from the stripping of ornamentation and 'bourgeois' details from structure. The term 'form follows function' is often used to summarise the Bauhaus approach. When Brigitte and Klaus emigrated to Australia from Germany in 1982, Klaus became Founding Head of the Glass Workshop at the Australian National University in Canberra, his influential teachings drawing on Bauhaus principles and transforming the course of Australian glass.

The couple, in turn, began a period of intense creativity, inspired by the beauty of their new surroundings, stimulated by the clarity of light and liberated by the sense of space. Their home is a reflection of experiences shared, informed in spirit by the predominant design movement of the last century and opening up in response to a new-found land, culture and lifestyle.

gateway
to a new vernacular

Sculptural arches in raw materials are the unusual gateways to this autonomous home – a collaboration between the owner, a retired academic and sculptor, and one of his former students, architect Tone Wheeler. The imposing 'entrances' reflect the owner's belief in honesty of construction with materials at hand. They frame each end of the house, a realisation of the environmental design theories that he once taught and still believes in.

'The arches are an aesthetic consideration', says the owner. 'They emphasise the long central axis and siting of the house to get passive solar energy – an extension of that form to nature. Several people said they looked like Japanese arches; I realised that during my three years in Japan the architecture had obviously had a subliminal imprint. The proportions of the arches were intuitively based on the Golden Mean – a concept learnt in my 20s. Every artist has a certain aesthetic; you can probably trace it back to the important influences in your life.'

The building is a home and studio for the owner and something of a prototype for sustainable living based on an innovative use of pre-fabricated materials and low-cost construction. 'Tone and I are interested in mass production', states the owner. 'Most architects deal with wealthy people and corporations; the mass housing that you see everywhere is done by developers and that, to me, is a sad situation. So this house is an attempt to bridge that gap. If the sort of thought we practised here went into stock homes for developers you could make better, environmentally sound habitats for their clients.' The architect agrees: 'We were looking for something that could go into ecologically difficult areas and be built simply and quickly without much work on-site. We want to make housing "plural", not a one-off mud-brick or rammed earth building'.

above: The louvres above the doors are set at a carefully chosen angle to allow the winter sun to penetrate deep within and to keep the summer rays out. In summer the louvres shade the glazing and ground in front of the doors.

right: 'This place has no contact with city water, sewerage, gas, anything', states the owner. 'The reed beds in front of the house are transpiration beds for the grey water from the sinks and showers. Next to them are the round septic tanks – everything that has a use remains visible.' The dam also has a use, functioning as a secondary water supply for the gardens and the emergency bushfire spray system.

following page: The partially covered walkway connects the living areas on the right with the bathrooms on the left. The tall exhaust columns aerate the dry composting toilets.

The site is depicted by the owner as a 'standard, dreary bush block with secondary growth, stunted things, crappy soil'. He considered the remote location 'a challenge to do something environmentally interesting. If you can do it here, you can do it anywhere in Australia'. The cool-temperate climate is wryly described by the owner as 'mediocre, it's never hot or cold and the unpredictable rainfall means it's not good tourist weather'.

The design responds admirably to all these factors. As the architect outlines, 'It is a fully autonomous home that generates its own power, provides for its own heating and cooling, harvests rainwater and recycles wastewater'. The long 'string' of living

rooms, with a separate wing for visiting family and friends, is orientated north, the roof tilted up for maximum passive solar gain in winter. The bedrooms and living areas are separated by breezeways and an enclosed herb and vegetable garden is next to the kitchen. The southern roofs of the two small bathrooms and larger carport/storage space are angled to hold solar water-heating and photovoltaic panels. A grass slope runs gently from the front of the house to a dam and the rear is dug (with minimal excavation) into the hill, the garden embankments and exterior courtyards thus more protected and benefiting from the winter sun.

'One of the things I liked about this site was the slope', states the owner, 'for I knew we would be able to make a visual play of the land and water. I didn't want any element of the man-made garden at the front of the house, I wanted to look straight out to the natural bush'.

A central 'corridor' runs the length of the building and all the rooms are reached from this. The walkway alludes to the old-style Australian vernacular, with its partial covering chosen by the owner, who, says Tone, 'wished to maintain contact with the daily weather patterns by continually interacting with the outside while still being protected'.

The architect states an intent to 'capture the spirit of a country house without being too literal. A modern, functioning home put together with a bushman-like feel – the wire and the posts giving a "farm" air'. There's certainly a utilitarian look to the spare structure, which is designed around a grid of 1200 millimetres to suit standardised, readily available components.

'The use of low embodied energy materials and modular, prefabricated construction reduces the demand for material resources', says Tone, 'and you can see the straightforward making of it'. The house acknowledges the distinct vernacular in Australia of rural buildings using logs, corrugated iron and 'fibro' (fibre-cement sheeting) for ease and versatility of construction. 'There's a tradition of building sheds with a minimum use of material', says Tone. 'An old woolshed can make a better-looking living room than most project houses. We like the idea of taking low-tech, low-cost materials and using them in a more sophisticated way to make things modular, factory-made and easily assembled.'

'These outside rooms', says the owner, 'have as much effort put into them as the shell of the building. So, the environment is not just about the house's orientation – it's solving all the problems, water, sun and, in this case, soil. We didn't even have soil, we actually had to make it. We used manure and composting'. Tone continues: 'I like the fact that we made "architecture" out of the self-sufficiency of growing vegetables – low-grade "architecture" but integrated pieces of the house'. The netted 'tepee shaped' garden references the form of an original, sustainable dwelling built many years ago by the owner's father.

Rainwater is harvested from the entire roof area for use throughout the house. There's a special dual guttering system that filters and removes all leaf material before water enters the system. The tank water is gravity fed, or it can be pressure-pumped to the taps and solar hot-water system.

'There's a visual connection between the water collection on the roofs, through the box gutter to the tanks and then back through the bathrooms to the transpiration beds on the north side. The owner and occupants can feel the water system flowing around them as they use the house', explains the architect.

above: All bedrooms have a vista across the reed beds and dam to the spotted-gum slope. In the evening contemporary technology replaces daylight. Fluorescent lights with efficient electronic ballast and starters are located in the pelmets to reflect off the Zincalume ceilings, giving even lighting.

left: In the living room/kitchen the floor slab, in common with all the rooms, has a coloured oxide topping for finish and remains uncovered to utilise the full benefit of the thermal mass. The living spaces each have a fireplace for auxiliary heating in winter, and the integral surround adds some convective heat and keeps timber dry and close at hand. The owner harvests firewood from fallen logs on the property: 'In the city, or if I had to chop trees down, I wouldn't have a fireplace'.

'The breezeways are a functioning environment', explains the owner, 'They help to create an acoustic division from one room to another and you can hang your laundry out in them. Wood and vegetables are also conveniently stored here next to the kitchen. I didn't put those racks there so that they would make a nice photograph!'

With home-grown food on the table, no shortage of water and an Environment Award in 2003 from the Royal Australian Institute of Architects, the house is clearly achieving its aims. Tone concedes that 'stretching the building to its very limits' actually resulted in too much heat in winter: 'Everything is warm except the bathrooms – it needs a cooler place for wine, computers and food stuffs. That's the lesson!'

For the owner this is a home for a simple, frugal life, in contact with the natural surroundings but with more comfort than the barn he had lived in for the past 12 years. Reflecting, he says, 'In the 1950s and 1960s you were thought a radical or extremist if you voiced environmental theories, but now everyone realises the industrial countries are using a disproportionate amount of resources. Today the educational system is making people more aware of it. What is here is what I used to teach as theory and I finally had the opportunity to do it on a very modest budget ... it's just fibro and tin, humble materials. So perhaps this is one of my final statements in life'.

The kitchen is fitted with built-in furniture made from
plantation-sourced hoop pine and some recycled timber.
The rugged table was devised and constructed by the
owner from a whole piece of reclaimed timber. The layers
of polycarbonate sheeting on either side of the truss
provide some double-layer insulation. The fibre-cement
walls and their fastening are left bare in keeping with the
unpretentious aesthetics. Also, the architect explains, 'The
seamless, hi-tech approach that makes things disappear
costs a lot, so all the construction workings are left on
display, making replacements and alterations easy'.

glossary

Adobe

Sun-dried earth blocks or mud bricks – usually formed by hand-puddling using a wooden or metal form.

Aerated concrete blocks

Lightweight all-purpose building blocks that are produced by adding a foaming agent to concrete and applying steam. Blocks can be cut and shaped easily, and have good insulation and moderate thermal mass. They have relatively high embodied energy.

Architects

Should we heed the advice of Alistair Knox who, in 1975, stated 'Architects can be visual and superficial rather than structural and fundamental. Choose a planner with his mind in the heavens and his feet on the ground'.[15] Since 1975 there have been an increasing number of architects practising environmentally sound principles, although it seems bizarre that we should have to list them as having those qualifications. It would be more appropriate to have the minority of architects who advocate unsound housing principles listed with a 'dangerous for your health' warning next to their names. This book may have given you some ideas on how to select an architect.

Cement

Modern cement originated in Portland, England, around 1824. Now made around the world, it is still called Portland cement as the ingredients remain the same: calcium, from chalk or limestone, together with alumina and silica, from clay and shale. The manufacturing process mixes and grinds these substances before high-temperature kiln-firing removes water. This process also fuses the ingredients into chunks, which are then cooled, powdered and mixed with gypsum. The result – a useful product for making mortar and concrete, but one high in embodied energy.

Cinva ram block press

One of the better-known makes of machines designed to compact earth into stabilised earth bricks.

Cob

A mixture of clay, straw and water; lumps of cob are pitched layer on layer to form walls. These can be smooth-finished. Common in the south west of England, it was also a method used by Australian pioneers.

Compressed soil blocks/bricks

These are created by compacting moist earth into forms by hand-ramming or power-pressing.

Dry composting toilets

These toilets function without the need for water or connection to mains sewerage. They rely on old principles of organic decomposition and an aerating ventilation fan to break down waste into a usable compost. Most makes have a chamber below the bowl from which processed material is periodically removed. One of the better-known brands is the Clivus Multrum composting toilet (www.clivusmultrum.com).

Easiwall

An environmentally friendly walling product made of compressed wheat straw with a recycled paper lining; it is said to offer fire-resistance, noise and thermal insulation, cost savings and many other benefits (www.ortech.com.au).

Embodied energy

The amount of energy needed to create a product. Earth, for example, is low in embodied energy; steel requires a lot of processing (mining, firing and shaping) and is therefore high in embodied energy.

Enclosed gutters

Roof gutters designed to keep out bird droppings, heavy metals and leaves, and prevent mosquito breeding. They are easier to clean than conventional open gutters. Several houses featured have used Enviro Flo Gutters.

Fibre-cement boards

Generally made from timber (radiata pine), cement and sand, these boards are durable, water-resistant and unaffected by termites, fire and rotting. Different varieties can be used for exterior cladding, bathrooms, laundries and other interior applications.

Fly ash

A waste product – the fine ash from burnt coal – also known as FBA (furnace bottom ash). Instead of going to landfill it can be used as a substitute for cement.

Hoop pine

A plantation-grown timber from Queensland, Australia. While there is some debate on how plantations should be grown and treated, they are the best option for the sustainable use of timber.

Insulation values

The thermal qualities of materials can be expressed in terms of R and U values. R measures a material's ability to resist temperature flow. U measures the ability of a material to absorb temperatures. Conventional homes often acquire a good R rating through energy expenditure and capital-intensive methods – for example, 'wrapping' the walls and ceilings in synthetic insulation materials high in embodied energy, and then pumping hot or cold air in to maintain a comfortable environment.

Off-gassing

The release of noxious fumes from materials, particularly in enclosed interior spaces. Formaldehyde, when used as a binder in particle boards, is particularly dangerous.

Passive cooling

Through the use of shading, cross-ventilation, rotating roof vents and other 'passive' methods of cooling a house, air-conditioning and other cooling devices costly to the environment can be eliminated.

Passive design

Passive design makes use of natural energy; buildings based on passive design principles minimise reliance on mechanical heating and cooling appliances.

Passive solar heating

The use of design to restrict the sun's access to a house in summer while allowing it to penetrate in winter. In winter heat is stored in dense building materials and kept within the building by insulation and attention to glazing.

Permaculture

Founded by David Holmgren and Bill Mollison, permaculture takes a caring, holistic approach, integrating gardening, agriculture, ecology, architecture and technology. Its philosophy includes working with the earth and nature to bring about sustainable living through the harmonious integration of the land and its occupants. There are many websites and books on the subject.

Radial sawing

This ancient and natural method of cutting wood dates back to Viking times and is valued today for minimising timber wastage (conventional sawing methods discard outer parts of the log). The milling process also applies to small logs and works with the stress patterns of the timber. Wedge-shaped slices and varying plank widths are produced (see www.radialtimber.com for more information).

Rammed earth blocks

These soil blocks are larger than bricks and are formed by ramming the earth manually or by a pneumatic drill. Whole wall sections can be manufactured off-site and transported.

Slag

A mining waste-product that often goes to landfill; it can be substituted for cement (high in embodied energy) in concrete, substantially reducing carbon dioxide emissions.

Sod

Renowned in Ireland and used by early Australian immigrants; strips of turf are used for walls and roofing (supported by sticks). Walls can be over a metre thick and are traditionally smoothed off to deflect rainwater.

Stack cooling

This method works on the principle of warm air rising to be replaced by cooler air entering below. The effect is accentuated by increasing the difference in height between the exit and entry points – for example, by having a 'tower' within the structure for the release of warm air and a basement area for the intake of cooler air.

Straw boards

An alternative lining board made of unprocessed straw, treated with borax and salts for fire-resistance. The boards provide insulation and good acoustics, and are also available untreated. One manufacturer is Solomit (www.solomit.com.au).

Thatching

All kinds of grasses are employed for thatching. In England, where there is a long tradition of thatching, rye, barley, oat and wheat straw have been used to form thick roofs giving both insulation and protection from the elements.

Thermal mass

Materials with high density, such as concrete and bricks, have good thermal mass – the ability to absorb and retain thermal energy and release it slowly at a later stage.

Vernacular architecture

A style of native or 'popular' architecture peculiar to, or connected to, a particular place. It takes into account the climate and available local resources – for example, pole houses in areas prone to flood, igloos in the Arctic, and adobe houses in Mexico.

Wattle and daub

A building technique dating back to Roman times. A lattice of twigs or rods is used to make a framework for the wall; a mud mixture, often including cow dung, is then daubed on both sides of the basket-style construction. The method was brought to Australia by early immigrants.

Wood fires

The use of wood fires for heating and cooking is an ancient tradition and an undeniable pleasure. However, while today's 'fuel-efficient' wood-burning stoves have reduced smoke emissions and maximised the storage of heat, we need to minimise our reliance on fires, which produce air pollution and greenhouse gas emissions. 'Found' wood is the least environmentally damaging source of fuel but even this practice affects the natural order. A study in Victoria, Australia, estimated that around 620,000 tonnes of firewood are used each year in Victoria (see www.dse.vic.gov.au for more information).

recommended reading

During the research for *Sticks, Stones, Mud Homes - Natural Living*, I perused hundreds of books and internet sites. The latter, often devised by enthusiastic owner–builders wanting to share their hard-won knowledge and tips, were a joy to discover. The world-wide web is a terrific source for all matters concerning ecological living and earth-building, and it's a good feeling to connect with other like-minded people looking for alternative ways to tread lightly on the earth. It seems something of a paradox that low-technology living is so well served and supported by a hi-tech medium.

In researching, part of the fun is the process itself, the way surfing the net invites exploration of eye-catching links and unlikely topics, so I have not actually listed sites – just go to your favourite search engine with the starting point of a few well-chosen phrases or topics.

The architectural and interior design sections of mainstream bookshops have surprisingly few publications concerning environmental living, although, as public awareness grows, many more titles are emerging. You may have to dig below the surface to unearth these alternatives – libraries are a good hunting ground. Here I have listed a handful of titles that have ended up on my shelves and are as good a place as any to start if you would like to follow up any of the ideas presented within these pages.

Alexander, C, Ishikawa, S, Silverstein, M, Jacobson, M, Fiksdahl-King, I & S Angel, *A Pattern Language - Towns, Buildings, Construction*, Oxford University Press, New York, 1977.
The owners of the straw bale house featured on pages 96–105 were inspired by this book – an early classic that empowers us to devise our own living spaces. Many of the ideas expressed are based on the good tenets of historic and vernacular houses. The fundamental philosophies remain sound although the passages on contemporary materials could be updated.

Baggs, S & J, *The Healthy House - Creating a Safe, Healthy and Environmentally Friendly Home*, Harper Collins, Sydney, 1996.
The authors of this thoroughly researched Australian publication have, between them, over 75 years of experience with earth-sheltered architecture. They take a holistic approach to designing and writing on healthy buildings.

Birkeland, J, *Design for Sustainability - A Sourcebook of Integrated Eco-logical Solutions*, Earthscan Publications Ltd, London, 2002.
A comprehensive source book that takes an academic but very readable approach to 'environmental and social problem-solving'. The list of contributors includes some of the most prominent figures in the field of ecological discussion and literature.

Brand, S, *How Buildings Learn - What Happens After They're Built*, Viking, Penguin, New York, 1994.
The author, creator of *The Whole Earth Catalogue*, an inspirational publication for an earlier generation, deconstructs and documents the aging process of buildings in a readable style, revealing fact and information with great insight. This book appeals to general readers, do-it-yourself enthusiasts and building professionals. The archive photos showing changes to buildings over the years are compelling.

Chadwick, W & I de Courtivron, *Significant Others - Creativity and Intimate Partnership*, Thames and Hudson, London, 1993.
David Fairbairn and Suzanne Archer credit this book as the inspiration for building their art house (see page 110).

Day, C, *Places of the Soul*, Thorsons, London, 1993.
This book is described on the cover as demonstrating 'how building design can start with people and place and how buildings can develop organically from these foundations – our surroundings affect us physically and spiritually'. An accurate summary of a heart-warming approach to natural architecture.

Drew, P, *Touch This Earth Lightly - Glenn Murcutt in His Own Words*, Duffy & Snellgrove, Sydney, 1999.
The author reveals the results of 40 hours of insightful interviews with the award-winning Australian architect Glenn Murcutt.

Edwards, R, *Mud Brick Techniques*, Rams Skull Press, Kuranda, 1990.
An Australian pamphlet-style book that clearly outlines the methods of making and building with mud bricks. The simple black-and-white illustrations are surprisingly effective.

Hollo, N, *Warm House, Cool House - Inspirational Designs for Low-Energy Housing*, Choice Books, Marrickville, 1995.
A practical guide with simple explanations on the principles and design of low-energy housing. It is aimed at 'anyone buying, building or altering their house', and written by an

author with much theoretical and practical involvement on the subject.

King, B, *Buildings of Earth and Straw*, Ecological Design Press, California, 1996.
This delightful and informative book was intended, admits the author, to appeal to the 'technical folks' (engineers, building officials, architects) and 'normal folks' (primarily home owners). In King's own words: 'This means that some of the information is going to be very useful to some of you and not so useful to the rest of you. Without sacrificing clarity or thoroughness, every effort has been made to juggle the information needs of both sets of people'.

Knox, A, *Living in the Environment*, Second Back Row Press, Leura, 1985.
A slim volume, originally published in 1975 by Mullaya Publications, it is written with passion and documents the writer's own struggles to forward earth-building in Australia. Knox also muses and philosophises on environmental issues and the value of living close to nature. (Currently out of print; try secondhand book stores or www.abebooks.com.)

Lawlor, A, *A Home for the Soul - A Guide for Dwelling with Spirit and Imagination*, Clarkson Potter, New York, 1997.
The title says it all!

Lazenby, G, *The Healthy Home*, Conran Octopus, London, 2000.
The author is strong on matters contributing to stressful living and offers measures to relieve this. Her definition of clutter – 'Clutter is anything that makes you feel down, depressed or sad when you look at it or think about it' – led to a review and downsizing of my collection of books, clothes and ornaments.

Minke, G, *Earth Construction Handbook - The Building Material Earth in Modern Architecture*, Wit Press, Massachusetts, 2000.
A fine practical book that describes in detail the various methods of building with mud.

Mobbs, M, *Sustainable House - Living For Our Future*, Choice Books, Marrickville, 1998.
Michael Mobbs documents step by step his family's resolve to transform an ordinary terrace house in Sydney into a sustainable house – almost entirely self-sufficient in power, water and waste disposal. If you buy only one book on how to build or renovate

in an ecological and sustainable manner, this must surely be your first choice; inspirational, practical and informative, it is far more than just the story of a house conversion.

Oliver, P, *Dwellings*, Phaidon Press, London, 2003.
The author first published *Dwellings: The House Across the World* in 1987 and this revised edition offers more insights and scholarly text on the subject of vernacular architecture. It is a timely release as much can be learned from vernacular architecture, which, as the book jacket informs us, 'represents in excess of 90 per cent of the world's buildings, including some 800 million dwellings'. This has become the essential bedtime book for myself and my six-year-old daughter, Summer; we both find the text and photographs fascinating.

Pearson, D, *The New Natural House Book*, Simon & Schuster, New York, 1998.
So many houses that I've visited recently have a copy of this book on their shelves. It was first published in 1989; the new edition is one of the definitive books on all aspects of eco-living, including the topics of energy, conservation, environmentally safe materials and the often overlooked aspects of health and spirit. It deserves the accolade 'classic'.

Steen, A & B, *The Beauty of Straw Bale Homes*, Chelsea Green Publishing Company, Vermont, 2001.
A visual compendium of inspirational USA-style straw bale houses covering a diversity of styles from Santa Fe missionary to individual 'turtle-shaped' guesthouses. The budgets range from low to expansive.

Suzuki, D with A McConnell, *The Sacred Balance - Rediscovering Our Place in Nature*, Allen & Unwin, Sydney, 1997.
Using insight, wisdom and fact, this book reveals our forgotten connections to nature.

Swentzell Steen, A, Steen, B, Bainbridge, D & D Eisenberg, *The Straw Bale House*, Chelsea Green Publishing Company, Vermont, 1994.
This densely packed, informative book from the USA is something of a touchstone for straw bale enthusiasts. First published in 1994 and reprinted in 1998 and 1999, it may be due for an update as methods of straw bale building continue to be refined across nations.

notes

1   William McDonough is internationally recognised and renowned as one of the world's leading environmental architects. In 1996 he was the recipient of the USA's Presidential Award for Sustainable Development. His ideas, articulated in writings, television appearances and speaking engagements, are very influential. For more information visit www.mcdonough.com.

2   P Drew, *Touch This Earth Lightly - Glenn Murcutt in His Own Words*, Duffy & Snellgrove, Sydney, 1999.

3   Australian Greenhouse Office; www.greenhouse.gov.au.

4   DM Roodman & N Lenssen, 'A Building Revolution: How Ecology and Health Concerns Are Transforming Construction', *Worldwatch Paper 124*, Worldwatch Institute, Washington DC, March, 1995, www.worldwatch.org/pubs/paper/124.html.

5   DM Roodman & N Lenssen, 1995.

6   S Brand, *How Buildings Learn - What Happens After They're Built*, Viking, Penguin, New York, 1994.

7   D Suzuki with A McConnell, *The Sacred Balance - Rediscovering Our Place in Nature*, Allen & Unwin, Sydney, 1997.

8   C Day, *Places of the Soul*, Thorsons, London, 1993.

9   A Knox, *Living in the Environment*, Second Back Row Press, Leura, 1985.

10   Alistair Knox was a highly influential architect and builder of earth houses in post–World War II Australia. His involvement with over 120 buildings and his articulation of the merits of mud brick led to wider acceptance of earth-building both in Australia and overseas. He struggled against attitudes, still prevailing, that mud-brick houses were inferior architecture and little more than huts. Although Knox died in 1986, his houses and writings keep his philosophies, idealism and affinity with the Australian bush alive. His son Hamish continues to build in Eltham, Victoria.

11   DM Roodman & N Lenssen, 1995.

12   Quote attributed to Laurence Doxsey, former Coordinator of the City of Austin Green Builder Program in the USA on the US Department of Energy website: www.sustainable.doe.gov/buildings/gbintro.shtml.

13   S Brand, 1994.

14   P Oliver, *Dwellings*, Phaidon Press, London, 2003.

15   A Knox, 1985.

16   A Knox, 1985.

contacts & credits

Pages 54–63
Mud mud glorious
Original design: Ben Hall
Extension design: Damian Barker and Debra Williams, 61 2 9810 9509

Page 65
The Immaculate Heart of Mary, Thurgoona
Design: The priests, inspired by a similar church at Margaret River, Australia
Draughtsman: Frank Percy, Albury, Australia
Rammed earth contractors, fabricators of the concrete lintels and saviours of the roof trusses: Anthony Wright, T/A Riverina Rammed Earth Constructions, PO Box 652, Lavington, NSW 2640, Australia

Builders: John, Pat and Brad Spinelli, 342 Diggers Road, Lavington, NSW 2641, Australia

Page 66
Building under construction
Designer and builder: Fergus Reilly, www.middlepath.com.au/temple/
Rammed earth contractor: Rammed Earth Constructions Pty Ltd, 90 Mountain View Road, Maleny, QLD 4552, Australia, www.rammedearthconstructions.com.au

Rammed earth samples
Courtesy of Earth Structures Pty Ltd; contact Rick Lindsay, 61 3 5778 7797, www.earthstructures.com.au

Small triangular window
Architect: Marci Webster-Mannison
Rammed earth contractors: Riverina Rammed Earth Constructions (details as per page 65)

Page 67
Barn
Builder: Hugh Krijnen, Braidwood, Australia

Pages 68–69
Charles Sturt University
Architect: Marci Webster-Mannison
Rammed earth contractor: Earth Structures Pty Ltd (details as per page 66)
Builder: Charles Sturt University

Pages 70–75
Organic matters
Architect: Gregory Burgess Pty Ltd, 61 3 9411 0600, www.gregoryburgessarchitects.com.au
Timber milling: RADCON – Andrew Knörr, www.radialtimber.com
Builder: Chris Irving

Pages 76–83
Bramare
Architect: Dennis Carter, Ward Carter Art + Architecture Pty Ltd, 70 Bull Street, Bendigo, VIC 3550, Australia, 61 3 5441 7855, design@wardcarter.com.au, www.wardcarter.com.au
Rammed earth walls: Earth Structures Pty Ltd (details as per page 66)
The Otis Foundation: www.otisfoundation.org.au

Page 85
City straw bale house
Architect: Paul F Downton, BSc BArch PhD RAIA, Principal Architect and Urban Ecologist, Ecopolis Pty Ltd, 105 Sturt Street, Adelaide, SA 5000, Australia, 0411 823 248, design@ecopolis.com.au, www.ecopolis.com.au

Pages 86–87
Hen house
Location: Ryde campus of the Northern Sydney Institute of TAFE, 250 Blaxland Road, Ryde, NSW 2112, Australia
Builder: Frank Thomas at Yesterday, Today, Tomorrow, 31 Parkes Road, Moss Vale, NSW 2577, Australia, 61 2 4869 3302, 0408 415 806, strawbales@bigpond.com, www.strawbale.com.au

Pages 88–95
Baled up in the Blue Mountains
Owners/builders: Shaina and Michael Hennessy at the Old Leura Dairy, 61 2 4784 1739, www.oldleuradairy.com
Architect: Rick Mitchell at Zone Zero, 61 2 4751 4762

Pages 96–105
Home truths
Architect: Andrea Wilson at Simpson Wilson Architects,

42 Chisholm Street, Greenwich, NSW 2065, Australia, 61 2 9439 5140, whimbrel@bigpond.com
Builder: Frank Thomas at Yesterday, Today, Tomorrow (details as per page 86)
Easiwall: Ortech Industries, www.ortech.com.au
Strawboard ceiling lining: Solomit, 61 3 9793 3088, www.solomit.com.au
Cushions: Cloth – new australian fabric, 207 Clovelly Road, Clovelly, NSW 2031, Australia, 61 2 9664 5570, www.clothfabric.com

Pages 110–17
Art house
Architects: Damian Barker and Debra Williams, 61 2 9810 9509
Builders/landscapers: Suzanne Archer and David Fairbairn, with help from Luke Sciberras, Ian Pickering on the walls and Ted Flapper on fixtures and fittings.

Pages 118–27
Coastal rock and roll
Architect: Thomas Isaksson, 61 2 9211 1903, isato@bigpond.com
Landscape design: Fiona Brockhoff Landscape Design, Sorrento, VIC, Australia, brockswann@bigpond.com
Dining chairs: Griffith Furniture

Page 131
Treetops, Tweed Valley, www.treetops.com.au

Pages 132–43
The house that Nat built
Designer/owner/builder: Nat Curnow, 61 2 4473 8673
Building assistance: Ian Wong

Pages 144–61
Sustaining family life
Architect: Clinton Murray, 61 2 6495 1964, www.clintonmurray.com.au
Building and concrete relief work: Andrew Murray, 0413 224 908

Pages 164–71
Sheds light
Artwork: Klaus Moje works available from Axia Modern Art, Melbourne, VIC, Australia

Pages 172–83
Gateway to a new vernacular
Architect: Tone Wheeler, 19/151 Foveaux Street, Surry Hills, Sydney, NSW 2010, Australia, 02 9332 1211, www.environastudio.com.au
Builder: Julian Barlow
Landscape architect: Sue Barnsley
Landscape contractor: Robyn Barlow

additional photography credits

Page 66
Building under construction:
Photo by Rammed Earth Constructions

Page 85
Straw bale townhouse:
Photo by Paul Downton

Page 117
Constructing the walls:
Photos by Suzanne Archer and David Fairbairn

Pages 118–27
All photos by Earl Carter, with special thanks

Inside back cover
The author:
Photo by Stephen Thaxter

acknowledgements

Since my formative college years, I have spent, and continue to spend, a working life playing the eternal art student – seeking elusive locations and beings that might stimulate, stretch and expand my visual vocabulary. The places featured in this book fit that 'elusive' criteria. They have been devised by inspired owners who have taken a long, exploratory look at how they would like to live. With ingenuity, resourcefulness and a fearless approach to design, they have brought about dwellings that are truly individual homes. Photographing their houses, interiors and gardens, and capturing the play of light on rough beauty, was an intensely rewarding experience and, as often happens in the process, increased my appreciation of the functional motives behind some wonderful forms.

What I hadn't expected to arise through this expressive mode of 'documentation', however, was a more fundamental self-questioning concerning notions of 'home' and how to make one. For this I must thank the owners, architects and builders for spending the time to share their guiding principles and for allowing me to photograph their hard-won discoveries and lifestyles. While this book bears witness to and draws ideas from their creations, it also aspires to add momentum to our collective search for eco-options in living and for a more holistic approach to home-making.

Acknowledgement is also due to everyone who gave invaluable counsel, spent time assisting with photography and generally helped to bring the book into being, with particular thanks to my publisher, Hardie Grant Books, and my commissioning editor, Foong Ling, for sharing a vision and daring to 'imagine'; to Alex for her knowledgeable and considerate editing; and to Simone who designed and directed the layout with an innate sense of balance and composition.

We could leave the last words
to Alistair Knox, who stated

'*The gnawing problem is how we can continue to multiply and till the land without destroying life as we know it, to discover how to live with it rather than in spite of it. The answer in a large part lies with the principles contained in environmental buildings increased many times, until it takes national dimension. Environmental building and environmental living are not a withdrawal from life, but a renewal of it. Neither is it a habit of fashion. It is belief in action.*'[16]

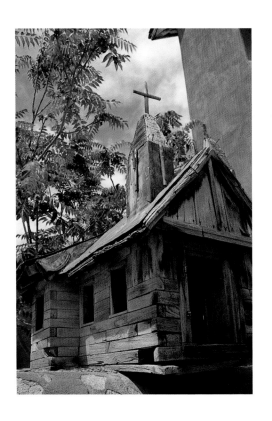

Published in 2004
by Hardie Grant Books
85 High Street
Prahran, Victoria 3181, Australia
www.hardiegrant.com.au

National Library of Australia Cataloguing-in-Publication Data:

Noyes, Nigel.
    Sticks, stones, mud homes: natural living.
    ISBN 1 74066 147 8.
    1. Architecture, Domestic –
    Environmental aspects – Australia.
    2. House construction –
    Environmental aspects – Australia. I. Title. 728

Cover and text design by Simone Aylward
Edited by Alexandra Payne
Photography by Nigel Noyes
Typeset by Simone Aylward and Pauline Haas
Printed and bound in Singapore by Tien Wah Press

10 9 8 7 6 5 4 3 2 1

Photo page 3: from 'Return to earth' story, pages 38–53.

The homes and interiors illustrated use methods outside
mainstream construction but it would be unrealistic to
suggest that this book is a manifesto for 'true green' living,
with every example adhering to the principles of safe and
sustainable housing. Virtually all building, particularly in
developed countries, will leave some imprint on the land,
and rare are the continuing, traditional aboriginal cultures
with dwellings that do 'tread lightly' on the earth. It would
also be unfair to the owners to present their houses as
'casebook' studies of a perfect ecological fit – they were
not necessarily built with that intention. In fact, we can
learn from their trials and errors as well as their many
successes and inspiring ideas.